Always add Love

Real Food for Picky Kids

Deidre J. Groehnert

Published: October, 2015

Always Add Love
Real Food For Picky Kids

Edited by Harris Fleming

Designed by Christopher Rubino

Content and Photography
by Deidre J. Groehnert

ISBN number 978-1-4951-7671-5

Table Of Contents

To Brenda!
wishing you many, many
wonderful memories in the
Kitchen! Happy Cooking!
Deirdre D. Woodward

Dedication

This book is dedicated to the generations who went before me, whose sacrifices allowed my family to have such amazing opportunities. Food connects us to our ancestors, and the traditions of their countries of origin. In my family's case, they lived in England, Ireland, Germany and Sicily before they came to the 'New World' to seek new lives. I honor them by sharing their food traditions and stories with my children (and hope to share with my grandchildren that are yet to come).

Acknowledgements

This book would never have been completed without the wonderful help and encouragement of my editor, Harris Fleming, and the creativity and design efforts of my sister Ruth Anne Dreisbach who, working with Katina Zulakis on her design team created the preliminary template and logo for this book. I also owe many thanks to Christopher Rubino for his invaluable contributions in design, which brought this book to the finish line. Thank you for your guidance and help with my first ever cookbook; I couldn't have done it without all of your support.

Where did the inspiration for this come from? Family, of course! First and foremost, I want to thank my grandparents, whom I miss dearly. Nothing encourages a little girl to follow her dreams more than the unconditional love of a grandparent! My best holiday memories include the tastes and smells of Grandma and Pop "Tini's" kitchen. I have very clear memories of the huge Thanksgiving dinners (see Grandma's turkey serving platter, right) and the intimate Sunday barbecues at their lovely house. I can see clear images in my mind of their backyard filled with apple trees, and can feel the breeze in my hair as I used to swing in their hammock and daydream.

After we lost Grandma, there were recipes we wanted to make, but couldn't find them written down anywhere (see Grandma's Applesauce Cake page 102), which inspired me to start documenting the recipes that could be captured from the family. I started typing out family recipes right after the birth of my twins, wanting to make certain to keep our family's food traditions alive for years to come.

It's from my grandma and grandpa on my dad's side that I get my love of making pies. Grandma loved making pies, and I can remember getting to drink sugary sodas when we visited her, which was a real treat. Family legend has it that they would decide how many pieces to cut into the pie, depending on how many people were ready to eat. If four people gathered, boy they each got a big piece of pie!

All my success is shared with the teachers I have had over the years. I am not formally trained, but learned in real home kitchens. My first cooking teacher was my mom, Jean Dreisbach; she lit the passion in me to create great, traditional family foods. Foods that have a lot of flavor, that fill the stomach and the soul. Mom taught me to always add love. Aunt Avis' mom, Marian, made us a needlepoint that said "Don't Forget to Add Love." It hung in our kitchen when I was growing up and now it hangs in my home as a reminder; it is the love that adds the best flavor!

I also want to thank the ladies who first made me excited about baking: Nancy and Becca Hall from down the block. I can remember making delicious cookies in their kitchen. Nancy was a lovely woman I looked up to, who left us too soon. She was from Louisiana, so we used a lot of pecans—still a favorite ingredient in my baking to this day. I started baking in their kitchen, and then began a lifelong tradition of baking Christmas cookies every year since I was young. I now make between 60 and 100 cookie tins and trays each holiday season, which I give out to friends, family and special helpers in our life (a cookbook of holiday cooking and baking is in the works!).

Growing up, I was fortunate enough to have lots of aunts, uncles and cousins around, many of whom also acted as mentors in the kitchen. I have special memories of sitting around the table, eating creations of my Aunt Joyce and Uncle Jim and enjoying Easter bunny cake and pumpkin pie cooked up by Aunt Polly and Uncle Bill. Now their boys Peter, Mark and Scott make the pumpkin pie. I have a tear in my eye remembering one special Thanksgiving dinner down in Florida cooked by Uncle Bob, Aunt Sally, Tommy and Silvie. Most of my aunts and uncles are not here anymore, so it is bittersweet remembering all of the fantastic celebrations we have shared in our

family. I believe that making the foods they made enlivens our memories and touches our hearts.

I was blessed to grow up in the company of so many joyful relatives who built memories around the table. Christmas celebrations with Aunt Grace and Uncle Joe, visits to Pittsburgh to visit Barb and Bill (first time I saw pulled pork) and summer parties at Aunt Carol's and Uncle Fred's house on Cape Cod. My then-boyfriend Steve and I had so much fun at parties at Ruthie's apartment in New York City; we felt like we were extras in an episode of Sex in the City as we sat in the corner observing all of the talented clothing designers, Wall Street wizards and all-around interesting party guests. Once Steve and I were married, we enjoyed many memorable meals around the table of his parents, eating fantastic British and German fare made by "me mum" Cynthia. I have a treasure trove filled with memories of great times with amazing people to call upon on a rainy day and, can't wait to make new memories cooking and baking with Ce-Ce and Anna, and Uncle Eric and Aunt Lindsay's kids once they can reach the counter!

Most importantly, I want to acknowledge my current teachers, critics and loves of my life: Steve, Tommy, Jason and Jacqueline. Their critiques make me a better cook, their crazy ideas stretch my creativity and their love and support has made it possible for me to finish this book (in between full-time work, soccer games, scout events, science fairs, piano lessons and all the other activities we share). I can just see Steve, sitting on the bench patiently while his nutty wife takes photos for her blog while dragging the family on yet another food adventure! He is my strong and compassionate better half, who takes care of us, makes us laugh, and shows us love and support every day . The high point of my day, every day, is spending time around the dinner table with these four amazing people, and it is for them that I keep cooking!

Thank you all!

Love,
Deidre

About The Author

I am not a trained chef, nor a pastry chef. I am a mom, a wife, and a businesswoman. Family and food are my passions and I want to let the world know that everyone can cook and bake. And that if parents make a conscious decision to cook real food, their kids will win in so many ways; they will develop a preference for real food, learn how to cook for themselves and associate tastes and smells with fun family memories.

Each day another form of fast food pops up to prevent us from using our kitchens. First it was the TV dinners of the 60s and 70s, then the "drive-thrus" of the world took over in the 80s and 90s, and more recently we have found ways to make overly salty and sweet processed foods that barely resemble real food anymore.

I want to lead a revolution back to the kitchen. (OK, maybe not an actual revolution; that sounds admirable but I'm simply too busy for that.) But I do feel like we are a bit at war with the unhealthy options out there; the easy road is paved with processed food choices. And when I am out and about, the single most common worry I hear is that parents don't know how to get their kids to eat (fill in the blank). Mostly, fruits and veggies are the hardest to convince their kids to eat. If it is a worry, we should get creative and find ways to teach them about real food. We shouldn't give up!

I get really annoyed when I hear that someone is in the house all day, and can't throw a few potatoes into the oven and bake them. The reward of knowing what is going into your kids' bodies; is worth a little effort. I work full time, and I had my kids—all three—in a span of 2 years (my older son was just 2-years-old and still in diapers when I gave birth to boy/girl twins). I worked almost every week from the time I

was pregnant with the twins through today, with only a couple of short periods off of work between jobs. I know busy. I now have three kids in grammar school, sports, music and scouts. We are all active in our church and love our neighborhood, friends and families. I continue working full time while I blog and write this book. Again—I know busy. I have simply chosen to prioritize a healthy diet in our house, and I believe if all parents worked on this, it would help improve the many health issues the US has, in one generation!

Feeding my three kids with their varying tastes, keeps me on my toes; to get them to eat real food requires some creative maneuvering around healthy ingredients. I hope some of my tips, tricks and secrets that have helped me win some battles in the kitchen, will also help you too. This cookbook is filled with recipes that work for picky kids, and tons of ideas for putting together tasty meals for weeknights. They can be made both quickly, and without breaking the bank. I hope they become a part of your rotation. I am a regular mom who is able to make this food in a small, outdated kitchen with little time to spare, so I believe you too can make these recipes, no problem! And once you master it, your kids will pick it up too. Pictured is a lunch one of my children made for me last summer when I was recuperating from foot surgery, not bad. It definitely made me smile!

"I've learned that people will forget what you said, people will forget what you did, but people will never forget how you made them feel"

—Maya Angelou

Introduction

A family dinner, cooked from the heart, makes everyone feel warm and happy inside. Food heals, it comforts and it unites. That is why I was inspired to share my favorite recipes with you! I want to help you not just get your pickiest of eaters to eat more real food, but also to share ideas for home cooked creations that will leave your family feeling loved, appreciated and confident enough to go out into the world and "crush it!"

I also hope that my passion for preserving family traditions for generations to come will inspire you to capture and share your family's traditions. It only takes one generation to lose the family recipes, so preserve them now, while you can.   I have been blessed with 4 amazing, loving grandparents (my maternal grandma is pictured above holding me). I miss each one of them all the time, and wish that through recipes I could recreate some of the tastes of my memories, but unfortunately many of their recipes left the Earth with them. That sad truth is common in many families, and this cookbook project began with the hope that I could preserve the recipes I do have from my family. And through my project also share them with the world, while inspiring others to save their recipes too! I especially love the quirky ways we use food around the holidays, and you will also notice on the picture above a little green Christmas tree with toothpicks stuck through shrimp, sitting next to the cocktail sauce for dipping. I mean, how cool is that? All it took was some Styrofoam and a little imagination.

I have a great love for family, as you can tell, but I also really enjoy cookbooks and have collected many over the years. I read them like a novel, eating up all the comments and background stories around the recipes and love to learn new tips and secrets. What I don't like is when I purchase a cookbook and only find one or two practical recipes I can use. I blame my pickiness with food, impatience for recipes that are too involved, and the fact that I am forever searching out recipes that will please my entire crowd with their varying tastes. So many cookbooks are beautiful and interesting but miss the mark for simple, tasty, and quick family-style cooking. These books spend most of their life on the shelf.

It is my dream to make a cookbook that has frayed corners, a worn cover, chocolate fingerprints, and sticky spills on many of the pages because it is used so often.

But I have babbled long enough . . . Let's get cookin'!

Proteins and Pasta

The following recipes are all straightforward and should take 30–45 minutes of effort, at the most. They have been scientifically proven to please even the pickiest of eaters (in the laboratory that is my kitchen, using my three very different kids as test subjects—see photo). Most of these recipes are for meals that you can make without turning on the oven, but a few of them will require only a short amount of time in the oven. If there is one thing my husband can't stand, it is when I crank up the oven in the heat of a summer afternoon. I included in the following pages the recipes that I could make at 4:00 in the afternoon in the middle of August, without getting into too much trouble for heating up the house and making the central air work too hard!

How I chose these specific categories of food had to do with my angels and what they liked, being budget-conscious and mindful of meals that could be prepared with little fuss. I also make suggestions of how to pair the proteins with veggies and carbs to round out a meal. Planning meals ahead of time is crucial when you barely have time to run to the market once a week.

I pretty much buy eggs, chicken, and ground beef every week, so I work hard to come up with uses for these basic proteins. Then, occasionally, when I see a great sale, I will splurge on a steak, seafood, or pork tenderloin. It is important to have a recipe ready at hand when a big sale hits the meat aisle.

I need my meals to be planned ahead and the shopping to go smoothly, starting with the toddler days when I had all three of the kids wreaking havoc in one of those ridiculous carts with the plastic car on the front. Not only was it a challenge to think straight so I could be organized, but those carts were the worst at turning a corner…I do not miss shopping with toddlers! At least now they can actually help out, which is really nice! And since they all have such unique tastes, I include them in the meal planning, which happens before you hit the register at the grocery store.

Hamburgers

INGREDIENTS

1 tbsp butter with a drizzle of canola oil

2 pounds ground beef (80%-85% lean)

2 shallots (finely chopped)

Salt and pepper

Ketchup and slices of American cheese

Cook the shallots in a small pot in the butter and oil for 3-4 minutes until tender. Mix into the hamburger meat, then form into 4 or 5 burgers. Salt generously on both sides, and pepper on one side (we don't love pepper so I don't do both sides; if your gang does, go for it!). Grill and serve on a nice toasted roll

Modification 1: Pizza burgers: To make pizza burgers, put shredded mozzarella on the buns and put them under a broiler for 2 minutes, or put a thin slice of fresh mozzarella on the burgers for the last couple of minutes on the grill to melt. Use my fast sauce (page 35) on them and voilà— pizza burgers!

Modification 2: Swiss burgers: Put gruyere or Emmenthaler cheese on the burgers the last couple of minutes of grilling. Cover the burgers with sautéed mushrooms or caramelized onions (just cook some sliced onions over medium low heat in some canola oil slowly for 20 minutes, with a dash of brown sugar if you want to encourage the caramelization). And if you happen to have some bacon around, always know that adding a bit of pork is never a bad idea; just lay a couple strips of crispy bacon on each to push it over the top.

Tips

Don't overwork the meat. I use one of those plastic presses to make sure that the patties are tight and won't fall apart on the barbecue grill. I take the advice from cooking shows and indent a thumb in each burger since they tend to expand in the middle. Don't smash the burgers on the grill or all the yummy juice is just being wasted! I used to cook my burgers well done, but now I have them medium rare; that one choice doubled the flavor!

• • • • •

We Love Grillin'!

Truth be told, my poor husband is sent out to the backyard in hot or cold weather, dry or wet, pretty much year round! When you have a husband who only makes pancakes and grilled meats, you find a way to have pancakes and grilled meats pretty much year round, certainly every week or two. It really helps to have someone else doing the cooking occasionally. But when the weather is warm, there is nothing we enjoy more than barbecuing and eating in the backyard together in the fresh air. Here are my favorite meats to grill, all easy and all delicious.

Steak *('nuff said)*

INGREDIENTS

Nice thick cut of T-bone or porterhouse
(purchase on sale!)

Generous amounts of freshly ground
salt to cover both sides of the steak

Freshly ground pepper on one side

Garlic powder for the other side

Rinse and dry off the steak, then let it rest 15 – 20 minutes to get to room temperature. Season well, then throw the steak on the grill and get those great grill marks on both sides. I can't advise how many minutes on each side; it will depend on the thickness of the steak and how well you want your steak cooked. Don't ever overcook, though; try for a nice medium for best flavor. I used to kill my steaks until I was shamed into the realization that the flavor isn't there if you cook it well done (see tips).

Put a pat of herb butter (page 6) on the finished steak right before serving, and that's it.

The T-bone and porterhouse are essentially the same cut and are carved from the same portion of the cow. Maybe best of all, both are two steaks in one: to one side of the bone running down the middle you have a strip steak, and on the other side you have the tenderloin (or filet). The tenderloin portion is larger on the porterhouses than on the T-bone.

Tips

You can always cook it longer if you find it's undercooked, but you can't pull it back if it is too well done. Learn how to tell doneness by the resistance you feel when you press a finger into the steak; the softer it is, the rarer it is. You want a pink and juicy center for the best flavor. It just takes practice and maybe a couple of burnt steaks before you really have the finesse to cook that beautiful, medium-rare steak.

Best served with campfire potatoes (page 85), peas (page 67) and salad (page 81) if you are enjoying an outdoor meal. For date night, kick up the elegance by topping with a few flash-fried shallot rings dipped in seasoned flour, accompanied by a nice fat baked potato and spinach (page 79).

You can save a few bucks getting a cheaper cut like London broil or flank steak, but I would recommend using a marinade on them or they will be a bit tough, and not as tasty.

· · · · ·

Herb Butter

INGREDIENTS

2 sticks of unsalted butter (must be at room temperature!)

1 tablespoon fresh herbs

1 good squeeze of fresh lemon; add the zest of a lemon first for even more flavor

Salt and pepper to taste (I add about 1 ½ teaspoon salt and ½ teaspoon pepper)

Put the softened butter into a medium-sized bowl. Add the herbs, salt and pepper. Squeeze in the lemon, avoiding the seeds.

Mix all together using a rubber spatula, then grab a large piece of clear wrap, mold the butter into the shape of a long cylindrical log and tighten the ends.

Throw it into the freezer for an hour or two and then you can keep it on a small plate covered in clear wrap in the fridge until you want to use it. If you don't need it that week, keep it in the freezer until you need it; it will thaw in only a couple of hours.

Grilling

I am not trying to be all "fancy schmancy" here; this butter will take only a few moments to make, I promise! You can make compound butter to add to rice or orzo, to put inside or on top of chicken cordon bleu, to spread on French bread or toast, drop on hot veggies or use to cook fish. The options are really endless here!

Tips

For the herbs, I like to use the following mix: half flat leaf parsley, a quarter lemon thyme and a quarter oregano for a chicken dish particularly. Rosemary is a strong flavor that works well with chicken or lamb and sage works best with chicken or pasta. The parsley, thyme, lemon thyme and oregano are mild enough for most applications; the lemon works particularly well with fish and chicken. Tarragon works well with eggs and chicken dishes.

• • • • •

Grilled Sausages

INGREDIENTS

Package of sausage (German bratwurst or sweet Italian are our favorites)

1 bottle of your favorite beer (I like Belgian beer and some of the new IPAs)

Cup of water

So simple, so tasty! Put the sausage into a soup pot and cover with the beer, then add as much water as needed to cover all the sausage well. Set the pot on high until it starts boiling, then reduce the heat to medium-high and set the timer for 20 minutes. Then just lay them on the grill, brown them on all sides and serve!

Grilling

Serve with campfire potatoes (page 85) and some beans (page 63)

Tips

I learned from my neighbor Yvonne that if you are having a party and have a lot of different things to cook you can do the sausage first and lay a clean, damp dish cloth over them and they will stay warm for a long time as you make the other dishes. It really works!

Also, I used to poke holes in the sausage so they wouldn't explode on the grill. I learned that you don't actually need to do that, though; I don't do it anymore and it seems to keep in the juices—and we haven't had one sausage explode on us yet!

• • • • •

Grilled Marinaded Chicken or Pork

INGREDIENTS

4 skinless, boneless chicken breasts
(or 4 boneless center cut pork chops)

¾ cup or so of olive oil (enough to surround the meat in the bag)

1 large orange (or 2 lemons or 3 limes)

4 whole cloves of garlic

6 peppercorns

1 tablespoon of sea salt

2 or 3 sprigs of rosemary

Handful of fresh thyme

Optional: ½ cup of dry white wine

Rinse and dry the meat, then pound it with a meat mallet to an even thickness, if breasts are very thick I cut them lengthwise creating 2 thin pieces. Clean and cut the citrus fruit into quarters. Squeeze the fruit into the bowl of a mortar and pestle with a splash of olive oil.

Put the fruit pieces in a one-gallon freezer bag with the remainder of the olive oil. Place the rest of the marinade ingredients into the mortar and pestle bowl (or some other vessel that will allow you to crush the herbs to bring out their flavors; the peppercorn and sea salt help to break up the herbs) and smash it all together. Once thoroughly smashed, pour the oil mixture into the freezer bag.

Place the meat in the freezer bag, zip it up and move it around to cover all sides with the flavors, massaging the marinade into the meat. Marinate in the refrigerator for at least 10 minutes, up to 2 hours.

Pat the meat clean with a paper towel and place on a plate, sprinkling a bit more salt onto both sides of the meat. Then, hand it off to your local grill master so he or she can work their magic. Grill until the thickest part of the breast is cooked through and white, but try not to overcook.

Grilling

Quick Weekday Summertime Meal

I use this marinade all the time! It is best with chicken or pork but could also work well with fish or shrimp. Lemon or lime can be substituted for the orange, although with chicken I really prefer the orange—it is the star flavor. When I add garlic with the chicken, it reminds me of Greek chicken. You can skip the garlic, however, if you don't have any in the house.

Tips

I suggest laying the flavorful chicken breast over a pile of homemade mashed potatoes, letting the marinade ooze onto and flavor the potatoes and accompanying with something crispy like lemon bean surprise (page 66). Since you are grilling anyway, you can serve the chicken with grilled eggplant (page 83). Another idea is to slice the chicken into strips and lay them on top of a nice salad (page 81).

• • • • •

Asian Marinaded Pork Tenderloin

INGREDIENTS

¼ cup soy sauce

¼ cup olive oil

2 tablespoons honey

Grated zest and juice of 1 orange

2 tablespoons grated, fresh ginger

2 garlic cloves minced

½ cup roughly chopped flat leaf parsley

1-2 pounds of pork tenderloin, cubed

Freshly ground salt and pepper

In a medium bowl, whisk together the soy sauce, olive oil, honey, orange zest and juice, ginger, garlic, and parsley or thyme.

Clean, trim, and cut the pork into 1-inch thick flat cubes. Season with salt and pepper, then put the pork into the marinade for 5 minutes. While marinating, soak the skewers in some water. Thread the meat onto the skewers and cook on the grill.

You can tweak this marinade to your tastes—replace the orange with lemon or lime, choose an herb of your choice to replace the parsley, or play around with the amount of garlic and ginger—but it's best to keep the balance of acid to oil the same.

Tips

Best served over rice, quinoa or orzo, with a side of carrots (page 71) or broccoli (page 78).

• • • • •

Pork tenderloin is a lean cut of pork that is fairly expensive, so when it goes on sale I can't resist buying it—even though it used to be that I wouldn't know what to do with it! Then I created this marinade, which has a hint of Asian flavors and keeps the meat tender and moist. Besides, serving food on a stick makes it fun for the kids! With pork, the only "watch out" is that it's easy to overcook the meat, leaving it dry and tough. To check for doneness, cut into a piece; you want the meat to be white throughout, but juicy.

Grilled Tilapia

Grilling

During a recent kitchen renovation gone crazy (the kitchen was only the start!), I had to get creative when it came to making healthy meals. I developed this recipe to find something new to cook on the grill, as the oven sat in the middle of the reno zone. I also needed to create a dish with minimal prep (since prep was happening on a chop board on the dryer in the laundry room!) This trying time of living through a renovation sets me up to really appreciate every aspect of a working kitchen, once it is ready to use, can't wait.

INGREDIENTS

2 fillets of tilapia

Salt and pepper to taste

1 lemon

1½ tbsp soft butter

4 or 5 fresh basil leaves

2 stalks of fresh rosemary

Clean and dry the fish. Sprinkle salt and pepper on both sides of the fish and lay it on a large piece of heavy duty aluminum foil (use a square big enough to fold over both sides into a packet). Cut the lemon in thin slices and lay them on top of the fish. Clean the fresh herbs and lay them on the fish as well (you can also use thyme, lemon thyme, parsley or dill depending on what you have available). Take the softened butter and pinch little pieces and put a few under the fish and the rest on top of the fish.

Wrap the foil around the fish like a little present, making sure to have all the sides sealed tightly. Cook on a medium grill for 10 minutes a side, then check for 'doneness'. The fish should just be white all the way through, if you see a little pink in the center, put it on the grill for another 5 minutes to complete the cooking. The fish should be moist, flaky and flavorful. Just transfer right to your dinner plates.

My eldest son, who has a sophisticated pallet, gives this recipe 2 thumbs up. It is one of those nice surprises when you sort of "wing-it" and end up with something good enough to add to a regular rotation of family favorites. The tilapia is mild, so the herbs, butter and lemon really shine! This serves 2, in my house we only have 2 fish lovers to cater to so the portion was perfect.

Nice served with some rice and lemon bean surprise (page 66) or ginger broccoli (page 78)

Chicken (or Veal) Marsala

INGREDIENTS

Dozen mushrooms (baby portabellas or button mushrooms), cleaned and sliced

2–4 shallots, diced

3–4 tablespoons of butter

2 tablespoons canola oil

¾ cup or so of Wondra flour (regular flour can be used if it is all you have)

4 large boneless, skinless chicken breasts

½–1 cup of Marsala wine (I just pour it in, I don't really measure)

Juice of 1 lemon

Small box of low-sodium or unsalted chicken stock (or use homemade if you have some)

Freshly ground salt and pepper

¼ cup heavy cream

Kitchen Basics® is a registered trademark McCormick & Company, Inc.

Wipe the mushrooms with a damp, clean rag or a mushroom brush; don't put them in water. Then cut them into thin slices.

Peel and clean the shallots and cut them into smallish pieces.

Put 1 tablespoon of butter and a couple of swirls of oil in a large pan (not nonstick; it is better to generate some lovely brown bits on the pan to deglaze later with the wine).

Put the flour into a re-sealable gallon bag.

The original inspiration for this recipe was something I read in a book of "365 MORE chicken recipes" (a gift from my lovely hubby). The title begs the question, "Why not purchase the book of 365 chicken recipes?" At 366, what is left? Surprisingly, there were some good ideas in this book, and what started as a standard recipe has evolved into a dish that is at the top of my kids' list of favorites (all three of them love it, which is a very rare meeting of the minds). Some nights I pair this with the Creamy Shrimp Over Linguini and let my husband and kids pick which they want over their pasta, and most of them take a bit of both.

Chicken (or Veal) Marsala

Clean and cut up the chicken breast into big bite-sized pieces, removing the fat and then drying the chicken. Season with salt and pepper.

Preheat the pan with the butter and oil on medium high just for a few minutes. Shake the chicken pieces in the flour, then remove them and shake off the excess flour. Place them in the hot pan. Don't touch them for a few minutes until they brown on the first side. You'll know the chicken pieces are ready to flip when they no longer stick when you nudge them; give them 2–3 minutes before testing, though.

BROWNING THE CHICKEN

Flip the chicken, then continue cooking until golden on the other side; remove to a dinner plate to rest. (They aren't cooked all the way through yet, but should be seared on both sides.)

Add another 2 tablespoons of butter and a splash of oil to the pan if the surface is dried out; be careful not to burn the butter.

Toss in the mushrooms and brown them for 3–4 minutes. Add the shallots and salt them right away. Sometimes I mince a clove of garlic and add it at this point as well, but it's totally up to you; that just bumps up the flavor a bit. Cook shallots (and garlic if using) for 2 minutes; by now the mushrooms should be nice and tender.

Pour in the Marsala wine and the lemon juice (no seeds, please!). Scrape the brown bits off the bottom of the pan as the wine reduces by a third (another 4–5 minutes).

Once the wine is reduced, add the stock and return the chicken to the pan and cook on medium-low heat until ready to serve. Because the chicken was coated in flour, the sauce should thicken; adding the cream later will also help to thicken the sauce.

Check the thickest piece of chicken to make sure it is white all the way through. Taste the sauce and add salt and pepper, if needed and the cream to thicken.

When the chicken is cooked through, you can add the linguine (or spaghetti or angel hair or fettuccine for that matter) right into the pan and finish cooking in the sauce. Or you can pour right over rice pilaf or even an instant white or brown rice.

THE VEAL VARIATION

For veal, follow same recipe but be careful not to overcook the veal or it will be tough. Veal cooks very quickly (especially thinly cut veal!); literally brown it only for a minute or two on each side and then finish in the sauce.

Any recipe started and finished on the stovetop is great in the summer, because you are not using the oven which heats up the house. This is also relatively quick, allowing for more time to play outside. I have given friends and family my recipe book over the years (when the babies were tiny, I took the time to type up a preliminary list of my favorite recipes and just gave it to loved ones) and this is the recipe most people make and let me know they loved. It has only a few ingredients and moves quickly!

Tip

This is best served mixed with linquini or over rice and on the side serve peas (page 67) or mixed veggies (page 75)

· · · · ·

Chicken and Pea Risotto

INGREDIENTS

2 cups bite-sized pieces of cooked chicken (or, 1 package of two large boneless, skinless breasts should be the right amount)

Salt and freshly ground pepper

1 cup cooked frozen baby sweet peas

1 cup grated Parmesan cheese

2 tablespoons unsalted butter

1 small yellow onion

6 cups homemade or store-bought chicken stock

¾ cup crisp dry white wine like sauvignon blanc or pinot grigio

Chopped fresh Italian parsley (the flat leaf one) if you want to garnish

1 ½ cups Arborio rice

Risotto generally scares home cooks away because of its well-deserved reputation of being a high-maintenance dish to create. It really does require a lot of stirring, but is stirring really too much to ask when what you are creating is so creamy and satisfying? I do all of the prep work ahead of time and surround myself with measured ingredients before I put heat under the rice so I can stick close to the pot to stir constantly. You might want to enlist a helper so you can step away and take a break.

First, prepare the chicken. If you're not using leftovers, brown whole boneless breasts on each side in a pan with olive oil, lightly seasoned with a bit of salt and pepper. Make sure they are cooked all the way through and then let cool. Once cooled, cut up the chicken and put aside in a bowl for later.

Cook the baby peas in the microwave according to the directions on the box, but shave off 2 minutes from the cooking time. Put them aside in another bowl.

Tip

To make the breasts cook quicker, cut them lengthwise like you are butterflying the breasts, but cut all the way through to make four thin portions from the two thick breasts. Then pound them a bit with a meat mallet.

· · · · ·

Chicken and Pea Risotto

Using a box grater or microplane, grate the Parmesan cheese and put it (yup, you guessed it) in another bowl or plate for later.

Finely chop the onion and put them aside, as well.

Measure out the stock and the wine, and you are ready to get started.

Now it is all about stirring, and is quite easy from here on out. Just make sure you can stick next to the stove for a while.

Put the stock in a large saucepan over high heat, bring to a boil and then reduce it to a very low heat just to keep it warm. Melt the butter in a large heavy pan or Dutch oven on medium heat. Add the onion and cook, stirring often, until the onion is softened (3 minutes or so). Add the rice and cook, stirring often for 2–3 minutes (until the rice is opaque). Pour in the wine, stirring and cooking until the wine is almost completely absorbed.

Stir in a ladle full of the stock, or enough to cover the rice barely. Continue to cook, stirring almost constantly, until nearly all the liquid is absorbed. Keep adding stock by the ladle full and cooking until almost absorbed for about 20–25 minutes. You will know you are done when the rice is tender but still firm to the touch. If you run out of stock, then use hot water. During the last 3 minutes, stir in the chicken and peas to heat through.

When the rice is just cooked, make a final addition of about 2/3 cup of stock or hot water so that the risotto is a creamy consistency.

Remove from the heat, stir in 2/3 cup of Parmesan cheese and season to taste with salt and pepper.

Spoon into shallow soup bowls, sprinkle with the remaining Parmesan cheese and parsley and serve immediately. Makes 4 main course servings or 6–8 first course servings.

This dish puts leftover roast chicken to great use; or, just heat chicken breasts like I show here. The subtle wine and Parmesan flavors combined with the creamy texture make it a sophisticated meal for a date night, while the overall texture makes it perfect for the youngest eaters. This can also be a vehicle to trick kids into eating their peas—everything soaks up the wonderful flavors, including the peas! The hardest part (as long as you prep ahead as advised) is to know for sure when it is ready to serve. You can tell by trying a grain of the rice; if it doesn't have much of a bite to it you will know it is ready.

Tip

This stands alone as a complete dinner, but you can accompany with some nice crusty bread and a salad (page 81).

· · · · ·

My Mom's BEST Chicken

INGREDIENTS

⅔ cup Wondra flour

1 teaspoon paprika

2 teaspoons salt

½ teaspoon ground black pepper

1 square or rectangular box of mushrooms (baby bella or your favorite)

3 tablespoons unsalted butter

1 tablespoon canola oil

3 cleaned, trimmed boneless skinless chicken breasts

¼ cup or so dry sherry

1 cup whole milk

¼ cup white vermouth

1 cup shredded Emmenthaler cheese (or Jarlsberg or gruyere)

Preheat oven to 350 degrees.

In a one gallon re-sealable plastic bag, pour the Wondra flour, paprika, salt, and pepper. Mix it around to combine the spices evenly. Take 1 tablespoon of the seasoned flour mixture out of the bag, and put it aside in a small bowl for later.

Tip

If you think you will need to cook the chicken in 2 batches, only put in half the butter and oil for each batch. If you have a large Dutch oven, put in all the butter and oil, since you should be able to brown all the chicken in one batch.

• • • • •

My Mom's BEST Chicken

Clean the mushrooms by wiping them off with a damp, clean dish towel, then cut them into 1/4" thick slices. Clean the chicken, trimming the fat and then cut into nice bit-sized chunks. When you are almost finished preparing the chicken, put in a Dutch oven or large, oven-safe pan with a lid over medium-high heat.

Shake the chicken in the bag of seasoned flour in batches, so that the chunks all get covered with the flour. Once the butter starts to bubble, lay the chicken in the Dutch oven/pan. Turn the chicken periodically to brown on all sides, then reserve the seared chicken on a plate.

Add the mushrooms to the Dutch oven/pan. Once the mushrooms are browned on one side (remember, don't salt them until after they are cooked or they will get tough) pour in the dry sherry to deglaze the pan, scraping up the brown bits with a wooden spoon—they're worth their weight in gold!

Let the alcohol in the sherry cook out for 3 minutes, then add back the chicken and pour in the milk and the vermouth. Sprinkle in the reserved tablespoon of seasoned flour so the sauce will thicken. Stir it around well and don't freak out if the milk separates a bit and looks curdled. Hang in there, it looks beautiful after it cooks for a while.

Put the Dutch oven/pan into the oven for 25 minutes. Open the lid, stir, add the Swiss cheese evenly all over the top, then cook for 5 more minutes without the lid.

Stove Top

The best cook I know is my Mom. I hope my kids think that about me, jury's still out! She knows how to season food perfectly, makes amazingly mouthwatering soups, stews and roast dinners. If I had to choose a last meal I would want my Mom's roast beef (end piece) with mashed potatoes and gravy; and, peas and carrots. Prepared well, it's as good as any top restaurant meal, if not better! This chicken recipe was another favorite of mine. Such depth of flavor as the 2 wines, milk, mushrooms and Swiss cheese play off each other so successfully. Now this recipe is in my regular rotation to serve the kids, yet fancy and original enough to serve to special guests!

Tip

Best served with rice to soak up the sauce, and string beans (page 63) as a crunchy element.

Me Mum's Lemon Chicken

INGREDIENTS

2 pounds boneless, skinless chicken breast cut into large chunks

½ cup of butter (or a bit more)

3 gloves garlic

2 lemons (zest and juice)

¼ cup cornstarch

Salt and Pepper to Taste

Fresh flat leaf parsley optional

Stove Top

My mother-in-law (aka "me Mum" since she is from Liverpool and is very cool) makes this dish for us when she visits. Most of the chicken and sauce recipes I make start with browning the chicken, this is interesting because the chicken cooks in the liquid leaving it moist and flavorful.

Clean, dry, trim and cut the chicken breast while you heat up a skillet (one that has a lid). Melt the butter in the skillet, then add the crushed garlic cloves. Cook on medium for only 2 minutes, do not want to brown the garlic or it will become bitter. Add the zest and juice of the lemons then the chicken breasts. Make sure there is enough room so that the chicken is not overcrowded. Put the lid on and cook on medium-low for 30 minutes, flipping the chicken over and stirring occasionally.

After the chicken cooks for 15 minutes, take a bit of the liquid and whisk it with the cornstarch to make a slurry. Then add that into the skillet to cook through for the final 15 minutes.

Season with salt and pepper to taste, and throw in some small pieces of fresh flat leaf parsley right before serving.

Tips

If you do not have enough liquid, you can add a cup of chicken stock or white wine. But if using wine make sure you cook out the alcohol by bringing to a boil for 5 minutes.

Serve over rice with a side of glazed carrots (page 71) or fresh and zingy mixed vegetables (page 75).

• • • • •

My Chicken Parm

INGREDIENTS

½ cup flour

2 eggs

2 tablespoon sherry or milk

¾ cup fine breadcrumbs (the restaurant version had ground breadsticks; you can also use plain bread crumbs)

¾ cup Parmesan reggiano

1 teaspoon dried Italian seasoning

2 tablespoon olive oil

2 tablespoon butter

3 large boneless, skinless chicken breasts (not chicken tenders)

Salt and pepper, to taste

Bag of shredded mozzarella, or grate a nice big chunk of mozzarella

1–2 cups of 20-minute tomato sauce (page 35)

Shallow bowls for dipping

Set up three dipping bowls, one containing flour, one containing whisked eggs and sherry or milk, and one with combined bread crumbs, Italian seasoning, and Parmesan cheese.

Clean and trim off all the fat from the chicken breasts, then cut them the long way in half (like butterflying them). Pound them as evenly and as thinly as you can. Make sure they are dry before you start dipping. (I use the flat side of my meat mallet to prevent ripping the meat. Cover with wax paper

My favorite dinner in the world used to be the chicken Parmesan at a local restaurant (though those meals would typically begin with a chocolate-tini and end with chocolate gelato and almond cookies). Then, one day, they changed their recipe and I was crushed! Who would change their recipe when they had reached perfection? I had to try to replicate it at home to feed my cravings. I definitely love my breaded meat (as evidence by my other recipes like Pork schnitzel page 47) but chicken Parmesan, done right, is the perfect indulgence!

Secrets:

Some important secrets to a fantastic chicken parm are to pound the chicken really thin, make a nice crisp breading and use a sweet simple sauce (page 35) and strong mozzarella.

or plastic wrap to avoid spraying the countertops with raw chicken.) Preheat oven to 350 degrees.

Start 1 tablespoon olive oil and butter heating in a nonstick skillet on medium high heat. Dip up to three breast pieces in the flour, then the egg mixture, then the bread crumb mixture and brown on both sides in the hot oil/butter. Put them into a baking dish and heat in the oven for 10 minutes uncovered to make sure the chicken is cooked through. Brown the other cutlets while the first are warming. Once the 10 minutes has passed, sprinkle on the mozzarella cheese and turn on the broiler for 1-2 minutes to get the cheese all browned and bubbly!!

Remove from the oven and warm the next set in the oven again on 350 degrees, then broil for 1 or 2 minutes to melt the cheese. Then plate all of the chicken cutlets and pour some sauce over the top and some extra to the side on the plate (see tips)

Serve with pasta. Pair with a fruit shake (page 111) for added health— but don't be disappointed if no one touches it with this in front of them!

Tips

Never walk away from the broiler, for any reason. Set a timer for 1 minute and check, then try another minute if it has no brown on the cheese. It is so easy to burn anything that is under that broiler—don't even run to the bathroom or you will have a charred mess.

I never put any sauce on until it is ready to eat, and even then you just put it on half the chicken. This is a restaurant trick so you don't overwhelm with the sauce or make it soggy; sauce lovers can always dip it in the extra sauce. Definitely don't bake it in sauce, or you will lose the crisp of the coating.

Grating the Parmesan cheese is fine, but if you can throw the cheese in chunks into a mini food processor or other chopping tool, with the bread crumbs, it helps make the cheese as fine as the crumbs and the breading cooks better.

• • • • •

Rainbow Chicken

INGREDIENTS

4 large carrots

12-18 purple potatoes

Bunch of asparagus

Large lemon

Large shallot

2 tablespoons butter

2 tablespoons olive oil

Freshly ground salt and pepper

2 large bone-in chicken breasts

1 teaspoon dried herbs de provence

1 large sprig each thyme and rosemary

Clean, peel and cut the carrots into large angled chunks. Scrub and cut the purple potatoes (little ones keep whole, medium sized ones cut in half and large ones cut into 3 chunks). Clean the asparagus and snap off the ends (where they naturally snap tells you how much of the woody ends to remove). Clean and cut the lemon in half, peel and clean the shallot and cut into 3 or 4 large chunks. In a small bowl melt the butter in the microwave, then stir in the olive oil with the butter. In a large bowl toss the carrots, purples potatoes and shallot in half of the butter/oil mixture and season well with freshly ground salt and pepper. In a medium bowl toss the asparagus in half of the remaining butter/oil mixture, also seasoning with salt and pepper.

I was home one afternoon, earlier than usual from work, and wanted to come up with a new and healthy meal for the family. I remembered how I have read that the more colorful foods are usually packed with nutrition (some exceptions are cauliflower, potatoes and bananas) so decided to start with the concept of packing the meal with color. The protein base for the dish was going to be chicken breasts, since they are a blank canvass. Luckily, I had a bag of purple potatoes (a random seasonal event that only happens around Spring and summer), a bunch of asparagus, a few carrots and a

Continued on next page

Rainbow Chicken

Clean and trim the excess skin from the chicken breasts, then take one half of the lemon and squeeze juice over the top of both breasts (do not discard the lemon). Pour the remaining butter/oil over or brush onto the chicken breasts top and bottom, then season top and bottom with salt, pepper and dried herbs. Brown the top of the chicken in the bottom of a Dutch oven over medium high heat with the lid off (takes only 3-5 minutes). Turn the chicken breasts over and let it cook on that side for another 2-3 minutes. Dump in the carrots, potatoes and shallot, squeeze the other half of the lemon over everything (use a small strainer to keep out the seeds or squeeze it through your hand to catch the seeds in your palm) and add both pieces of lemon into the pot. Throw in your fresh herb sprigs to add even more flavor. Put on the lid and cook for 20 minutes. Open the lid and toss the potatoes and carrots, then add in the asparagus on top. Put the lid back on and return to the oven for another 15 minutes. Open the lid and mix the veggies around some more and check the internal temperature of the thickest part of the chicken breast. It has to read at least 165 degrees, then you will know they are ready. Depending on thickness of the chicken breasts it may take another 10 minutes to cook the meat properly.

When ready to serve, remove the chicken to a platter to rest, covering with aluminum foil. Use a slotted spoon to get all the veggies out and onto a platter (discarding the lemon and herbs). If you want to make a quick sauce, the drippings are already flavored with the herbs and lemon, so you only need add a little chicken stock or white wine. Then add in some ice cubes and shake in Wondra flour to thicken (you want to lower the temperature of the sauce while you thicken with the flour), heat over medium heat for 10 minutes and you are ready to serve.

Continued from previous page

big fat lemon. That combination looked beautiful just sitting on the cutting board so I was sure this would be a winner! Cooking them altogether in the Dutch oven with a lid on top, helped all of the flavors soak into each other. The squeezed lemon, herbs and shallot generated a wonderful sauce at the base of the Dutch oven. I would definitely make this one again!

Tips

If you don't have 'Wondra flour', whisk regular all-purpose flour with equal parts of cold water, and use that to thicken the sauce.

Best served with crusty sour dough bread or brown rice to mop up the sauce

· · · · ·

Creamy Shrimp Over Linguini
WITH FLOUNDER SURPRISE

INGREDIENTS

12 deveined and shelled large shrimp

1 piece of flounder, cut into small chunks

2 tablespoons olive oil

2 gloves of garlic, diced

Zest of 2 large oranges (you'll squeeze in the juice later)

1 tablespoon butter

1 tablespoon Wondra flour

½ cup heavy cream (or more, depending on how much liquid you have for the pasta)

Salt and pepper, to taste

Half pound whole wheat linguini or spaghetti

Shrimp and white fish (flounder)

Heat a large pot of water for the pasta. While it is coming to a boil, chop your garlic, zest and juice your oranges, and line up the rest of the ingredients—butter, Wondra flour, cream, salt and pepper.

When you drop the pasta, start the shrimp—this will move very quickly. Set a timer to cook the pasta for 1 minute less than instructed; you will finish cooking it in the sauce.

Stove Top

OK, I admit this one sounds odd, but my father, husband and son all count it among their favorites, so there you go. As with so many good inventions, it sort of evolved from a mother's exasperation.

My son and I were in the fish section of the supermarket, picking up shrimp when he requested to add fish to our shrimp recipe. That made no sense to me, but I'm a strong proponent of letting our kids try things and learn from experience (ie, I was too tired to fight him). Flounder was on sale, so I bought a dozen large deveined shrimp and one piece of flounder.

Continued on next page

Creamy Shrimp Over Linguini WITH FLOUNDER SURPRISE

The main ingredients

As I said, this will move quickly so I suggest reading the rest of the steps before you start:

1. Heat a large skillet over medium-high and add the olive oil

2. Once the pan is hot, sauté the garlic for 1–2 minutes; don't let it brown or it will get bitter

3. Add the shrimp and flounder and cook for 2–4 minutes or until the shrimp gets an orange tinge

4. Pour in the orange juice and zest, add the butter and shake in some Wondra flour (before the sauce is heated, or it will clump). Heat, stirring constantly for another 2–3 minutes.

5. Pour in the cream and add the salt and pepper. Keep warming over low heat until the pasta is finished.

6. Pour in the pasta, stirring it in the skillet with the sauce and the fish. If there isn't enough sauce for the noodles, add more cream; if there isn't enough pasta for the sauce, that is what the bread is for—to mop up the extra sauce!

Stove Top

Continued from previous page

(I always get the shrimp deveined so I don't have to pull that gunk out myself, leaving me with hands that smell like the sea for hours.) We took our groceries home and got cooking. This was the resulting dish. (Did I mention my dad, husband and son said it rocked?)

Tagliattele Alfredo with Chicken

INGREDIENTS

1 ½ cup fresh Parmesan reggiano cheese

1 package of boneless, skinless chicken breasts

½ cup Wondra flour

2 tablespoons olive oil

2 packages of fresh tagliatelle pasta

1 stick of butter (I know, but I never promised you a thin waistline)

Salt and pepper, to taste

Stove Top

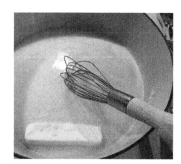

Grate the cheese and put aside for later (things move very fast in this recipe so you want to have it ready to go!). Rinse the chicken breasts, then pat dry and trim off the fat. Season with salt on both sides and cut into bite-sized pieces.

Heat the olive oil over medium-high heat in a large skillet, and start heating water in a pasta pot.

Put Wondra flour in a 1 gallon, re-sealable plastic bag. Add the chicken pieces to the flour and shake to coat on all sides.

Once the pasta water is boiling, add enough salt so that the water would taste like sea water, about 1–2 tablespoons.

Brown the chicken pieces in the skillet of oil. Don't turn them until the first side is browned (about 3-4 minutes on the first side, then 2–3 on the second side.) Reserve.

Cook the pasta for 1 minute, then quickly drain (if using dried pasta, cook it 1 minute less then recommended). Put 1 cup of the pasta water into a large Dutch oven or pot and heat over a medium flame. Add the butter and 1 cup of the cheese, whisking while the butter melts. It takes only a couple of minutes to melt the butter and create the sauce!

Dump in the pasta and chicken, stirring well and heating through for 2 more minutes.

Now you're ready to serve; just sprinkle in the rest of the cheese, shake in about a half teaspoon of pepper and salt (then taste for seasoning and add more as needed) and pour into a large serving dish.

This is super fast and perfect for a weeknight. If you want to encourage vegetable consumption, stir in broccoli florets—or, if you want to be diplomatic, you can serve it on the side instead. You can also throw in some frozen baby peas 4 minutes before the cooking is complete. Finally, I found a meal that all three kids will eat!

Tips

Gallon-size re-sealable plastic bags are very useful in the kitchen. I use them to marinate meats by pouring in my marinade ingredients, then adding my meat and mixing it around. I also use them to freeze cookies and pieces of bread and, as in this recipe, they make a great vessel to coat chicken in flour!

· · · · ·

Penne Vodka

Stove Top

INGREDIENTS

1 large onion, finely chopped

2 cloves of garlic, minced

2 tablespoons olive oil

2 large cans crushed tomatoes (I like San Marzano)

4–6 fresh plum tomatoes, crushed

¼ to ½ cup vodka

1 bay leaf

1 tablespoon finely chopped fresh Italian flat leaf parsley (or fresh basil)

¼ to ½ cup heavy cream (enough to make the sauce a nice orangey pink color)

Freshly ground salt and pepper, to taste

¾ cup fresh mozzarella in small cubes

1 package of penne pasta

Warm the olive oil in a large saucepan, then add the onions and sweat for 3 minutes. Add the garlic and heat for another 1 minute (never brown the garlic or it gets bitter!).

Add the crushed tomatoes and crushed plum tomatoes, vodka and bay leaf; stir. Warm over medium heat, stirring often, for about 25 minutes. Add the cream, parsley or basil, salt and pepper to taste and cook for 5 more minutes on medium heat.

Remove half of the sauce and reserve for another night, or freeze for another week.

Pour the cooked and drained pasta (remember, cooked 1 or 2 minutes less than the package states) into the pot of sauce that's left.

Add the mozzarella cubes to the pot of sauce and pasta and mix well, warming it for 2 minutes. Plate the penne (and add a bit more sauce from your reserved if it looks like it needs it).

This recipe has evolved over the years. I started way-back-when by asking a butcher what goes into vodka sauce; I took his advice and continued to refine my version as I went.
I get inspiration when I eat out to try and replicate dishes. Once, at a local high-end deli/caterer, I had ziti filled with fresh mozzarella cubes. Yummo! That inspired me to add fresh mozzarella to my penne vodka.
This has evolved into a lovely sauce and a family favorite for a meatless meal and—bonus!—it can be put together in 30–40 minutes.

Tips

This recipe can also be made more colorful by adding some frozen baby peas to warm up for the last few minutes of cooking, or by adding in a bit of red pepper flakes. Serve with a fresh fruit cup (page 96) or shake (page 111) on the side for added nutrition.

· · · · ·

Quick 20-Minute Tomato Sauce

INGREDIENTS

Small yellow onion, diced

2 cloves garlic, diced

Heaping cup of fresh cherry tomatoes

1 24-ounce can of whole tomatoes (I use San Marzano), cut roughly with kitchen shears or a knife

Freshly ground salt and pepper

1 tablespoon fresh basil, chopped (if using for spaghetti or chicken/eggplant parm)

1 tablespoon fresh oregano, chopped (if using for pizza)

Pinch of red pepper flakes (optional, if you like it hot)

Salt and pepper to taste

Stove Top

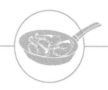

A super quick sauce that can be used for spaghetti, pizza, or on chicken or eggplant Parmesan. This sauce is so quick and tastes so much better than jarred sauce, you have to give it a go!
If you don't think it's worth spending 20 minutes to have freshly made sauce every time your taste buds demand it, double or triple the measurements and you can make a bunch of dinners for the future in about 30 minutes (it just takes a bit more chopping)! Freeze some of the sauce, and pull it down a day or two before you want to use it. Portion it properly for full dinners and you are all set.

Remove the stems from the tomatoes and squeeze out some of the seeds.

Add olive oil to a nonstick pan and heat for a couple of minutes over a medium-high flame. Add the onions, salt them, (and a few red pepper flakes if you like it spicy) and heat for 3 minutes. Then add the garlic and heat for another 1–2 minutes.

Add the cherry tomatoes and the whole tomatoes. Cook while stirring frequently for 10 minutes (or more if you have the time), and add the herbs, salt and pepper, to taste. Pour the sauce in a big bowl and use an immersion blender to make it into the correct smooth consistency.

If you don't have an immersion blender you can use a regular blender or food processor before you pour the sauce into the bowl.

Sauce is ready to go! Add hot pasta and stir, layer it on eggplant or chicken cutlets (page 22), or spoon it on pizzas (page 36).

Tips

As mentioned before, do not use aluminum foil when storing tomato sauce, unless you put clear wrap under it. The acidity of the tomatoes will eat holes in the foil.

• • • • •

Pizza Muffins

INGREDIENTS

6 English muffins (Wolferman's work the best—they are so thick it is like a Sicilian English muffin pizza)

1 cup pizza sauce (see 20 minute sauce, page 35)

1–1 ½ cups shredded mozzarella (full fat or skim)

Sprinkle of garlic salt for each muffin

Sprinkle of dried oregano for each muffin

A bit of freshly shredded Parmesan (optional)

Lightly toast the muffins and then put them onto a cookie sheet. Spoon sauce onto each, cover with cheese, sprinkle on garlic salt and oregano (smashing it in your palm first to release the flavor).

Cook under the broiler for 1–2 minutes or until the cheese starts to brown and bubble.

Stove Top

Here is an amazingly quick little appetizer or lunch to make with the kids. They will enjoy assembling them at almost any age. I make a large pot of tomato sauce or meat sauce once every month or two and freeze small containers that can be pulled down a day ahead to thaw and use on these pizza muffins. Homemade sauce elevates these and makes them a bit more nutritious.

Tips

Toppings can be added before you put these under the broiler. I've tried Italian sausage (out of its casing and browned in a skillet), cooked meatballs cut into thin slices, pepperoni slices, or caramelized onions, just to name a few. You can also use fresh mozzarella instead of the shredded kind, but it tends to be a little watery.

· · · · ·

Pasta Purses

This isn't so much of a recipe as a discovery! Recently I went to Kings supermarket (don't tell my husband, that store is very pricey!) and found these cool little pastas. They are like small little purses stuffed with Parmigiano reggiano. I served them with my vodka sauce (page 33) or quick 20 minute sauce (page 35), as well. They cook so fast—just boil the water and cook for 3 minutes. Perfect for a weekday! Two boxes made enough to feed the family, just supplemented with some garlic toast and raw baby carrots.

Tips

Look in your grocery store for perline. On the package they recommend a butter sauce, but I never like butter sauce on pasta; the tomato sauce was a nice sweet complement to the rich pasta.

Great served with pizza muffins (page 36) for a fun Italian dinner. Add a healthy shake (pages 111-115) to round out the nutrition.

· · · · ·

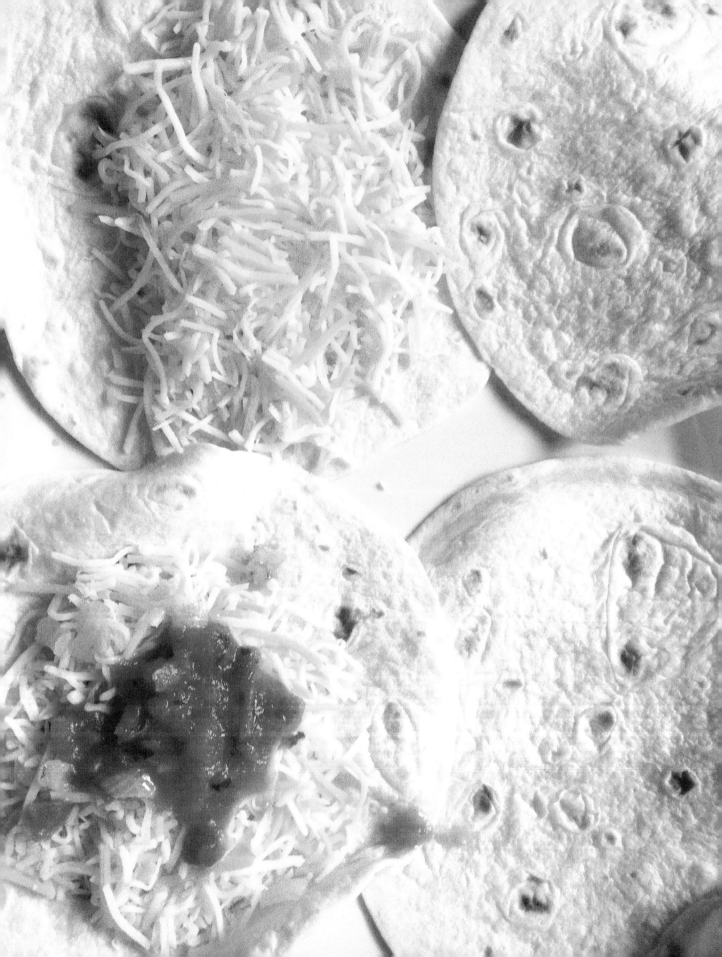

Mexican Night – Part 1

INGREDIENTS

2 pounds or so of 85% ground beef

1 small yellow onion or half of a medium onion, small dice

¼ cup medium salsa (I like anything all natural, but a favorite is Tostitos restaurant style)

¼ cup corn starch

1 cup water

2 shakes of oregano

3 shakes of garlic powder

3 shakes of Paprika

6 shakes of Mexican chili powder

2 teaspoon salt

½ teaspoon pepper

Dice the small onion and add it into a nonstick pan with the ground beef and salsa (no oil necessary). Heat it over med-high heat moving the meat around and breaking it up frequently until the meat is browned all the way through. Use a lid and dump out most of the grease into a bowl to cool (don't pour hot grease into a garbage bag or it will melt holes into the bag).

Put the pan back on the heat , shake corn starch on the meat and pour in the water, then add all of the seasoning.

Stove Top

One meal I am willing and able to throw together on a work night, is a Mexican do-it-yourself taco bar. The core of this meal is a quick 10 minute seasoned beef, the rest is just slicing and pouring all the sides and toppings into bowls. If I have a little extra time I will also make some Quesadillas (page 41), if I have rice in the house I will make rice, if not I will cook up some frozen kernel corn and peas as the side dishes and call it a day.

Tip

Most of the taco kits include a seasoning packet, if using add it in with the water. I throw them away and choose my own seasoning since the packet ones are very high in sodium and probably have preservatives as well. I would prefer to pick the combination of seasonings myself anyway.

• • • • •

Mexican Night – Part 1

Mix everything together and heat for another minute. Taste for seasoning, adding more of anything you think is lacking, and then the meat is ready to serve. Accompany with soft taco shells warmed in microwave for 30 seconds, hard shells warmed in a 350 degree oven for 5 minutes and/or nacho chips warmed in the oven for 10 minutes at 350 degrees.

Some food that can be used to fill your tacos or pile on your nachos or eat on the side are listed below (these are just suggestions, see what you have in the house that matches the Mexican theme):

1. Romaine lettuce sliced in thin strips
2. Tomatoes sliced in small cubes
3. Sour Cream
4. Shredded Mexican cheese mix
5. Salsa
6. The packet of sauce included in the taco kit
7. Baby peas and kernel corn
8. Rice
9. Sautee some diced bell peppers or if daring slice up some jalapeños

I provide the raw materials and the family puts together their own soft and hard tacos or nacho platters. To bump up the nutrition we always serve with cut fruit and baby carrots, or make fruit smoothies. Last night a friend of my son came over for Mexican night, and he found that salsa covered banana slices tasted great - now officially called 'spicy bananas'! I always find that it is good to let kids experiment (as long as it doesn't create a disaster in the kitchen!)

Mexican Night – Part 2

INGREDIENTS

1 tablespoon canola oil

2 tablespoons butter

Half of 1 small onion diced

Pinch of salt

14 soft taco shells (makes 7 quesadillas)

1 package shredded Mexican cheese (choose one with a mix of 3 types of cheeses, but without seasoning so you can control the flavors)

½ cup of salsa (I like Tostitos restaurant style medium or any all natural salsa that looks good)

Melt 1 tablespoon butter in a very small pot, once bubbling add in the diced onions and sprinkle with salt. Cook over med-low heat until the onion is soft, if it browns a bit that is fine...should only take 4-6 minutes.

Put 1 tablespoon each oil and butter in a large non stick pan and warm over med-high heat. While it is heating compose your first quesadilla on a plate. Layer a soft shell first with a big pile of cheese, and then spoon on salsa to taste and drop a pinch of the onions on top. For the pickiest eater I have to make a version with just cheese and wrapper (boring!)

Place this on the hot butter and oil, top with another soft shell and smash with, well, I don't know what to call it. You could probably weigh it down

Another quick item I make that can be a part of Mexican taco bar (page 39) night or just a stand alone appetizer or part of a meal, is the quesadilla. So easy and versatile, below I have the basic recipe but to this you can add yellow or red bell pepper chunks (just soften them first by sauteing in some canola oil) or jalapeno pepper diced if you like it spicy. You can make your own fresh salsa with chopped tomato, onion, cilantro and pepper; but, for the truly fast and easy version - use your favorite all natural salsa.

Tip

Dipping sauces like salsa, sour cream and guacamole can be served with these. If you are making a meal out of it, serve with rice and beans or make it a part of a Mexican taco bar night.

• • • • •

Mexican Night – Part 2

Stove Top

Chicken Quesadillas

- Clean, trim and cut 1 pound of boneless, skinless chicken breasts into long slim strips.

- Season the chicken strips liberally with salt, pepper, paprika, garlic powder and Mexican chili powder.

- Add 1 tbsp each canola oil and butter to a non stick pan, heat on med-high heat until bubbly.

- Place the strips into the bubbling skillet (don't overcrowd the pan) and leave them for 3 minutes the first side, then turn them.

- Cook the other side another 2-3 minutes, or until the meat is cooked all the way through.

  Add the chicken to the preceding recipe when you are layering the cheese, salsa and onions.

Tips

Test one of the strips by cutting the thickest part and make sure there is no pink in the middle, should be white through out.

· · · · ·

with a plate, but I use this tool to smash the quesadilla (and also for grilled cheese):

Cook on each side until the quesadilla is browned. When in doubt, flip it over and check the coloring. Place the completed quesadillas on paper towels to get the grease off of them. When you have completed cooking all of the quesadillas, cut them into triangles with a pizza slicer (not until they have set for a few minutes or the cheese will ooze out), then serve warm.

If you are making a bunch of quesadillas, as each is complete, keep it in a warm oven at 200 degrees until they are all ready to serve at the same time.

Dinner Pies
APPETIZER, BREAKFAST OR LUNCH AS WELL!

Stove Top

INGREDIENTS FOR TWO PIES

2 baking potatoes peeled, small dice

Pinch each salt, pepper and paprika to season the potatoes

1 onion, small dice

2 cups half-and-half (or heavy cream)

6 eggs

4 pinches kosher salt

2 pinches of freshly grated nutmeg:

2 Pillsbury Pie shells

2 cups of grated cheese of your choice (see page 44 for ideas)

Fillings of your choice (see page 44)

Preheat oven to 350 degrees. Take the pie crust out from the refrigerator to come to room temperature (or make your crust if you have an easy, reliable recipe!)

Peel the potatoes, and then cut into little squares. Heat 1 tbsp each butter and oil in a pan, and then add the potatoes with onion in small diced pieces (half a small onion per pie). Add a bit of salt, pepper and paprika to the onions and potatoes, and stir them around occasionally while you prepare the rest of the ingredients. Keep them cooking until the onions are tender, the potatoes have browned slightly and are basically tender as well.

I hate to use any shortcuts that include products that contain preservatives or weird ingredients, but I still haven't found a quick and reliable pie crust so I use Pillsbury 9 inch pastry shells for this recipe. They come in long boxes of two and usually can be found near the eggs.

As per usual, I always make two pies at a time, since it takes about the same amount of time and we get two meals from my efforts. Our favorites fillings* are listed on page 44. You can use whatever you have left over from the dinner the night before, within reason – it needs to go well with eggs (pretty much a blank canvas actually) and be cooked already or something that cooks quickly. Some specific leftovers that work well include cooked ham, broccoli or cauliflower.

Dinner Pies

Grate the cheese and prepare the fillings. In a large bowl whisk the eggs with the 'half and half' and then add the salt and nutmeg.

Put the pie crusts into the bottom of 2 pie dishes, then use your forefinger and thumb to crimp the edges. Put the cheese in the bottom of the pie evenly, then the toppings next, including the potatoes and onions. Pour the whisked egg mixture slowly over and between the fillings.

Any one of the following combinations taste great together:

*Cooked bacon cut into in small bits, cheddar cheese (definitely add the potatoes and onion with the bacon, you need the potatoes for volume, the bacon is small but flavorful)

White cap or cremini mushrooms sliced (don't need to cook ahead if you slice them thinly) and gruyere cheese or Parmesan cheese

**Frozen spinach and Jarlsberg or Emmenthaler cheese, this goes well with bacon for a little extra flavor.

Some other ideas for fillings are anything you would put into an omelet like cooked sausage and mozzarella, or diced bell peppers and serve with a little salsa on the side for instance.

The eggs will expand upon cooking. To be safe put the pies onto a cookie sheet in case there is any spillage. Bake the pie until it is firm to the touch like set Jell-O, about 45 minutes (I always check it around 30 minutes).

Cool the pie for at least 15 minutes before slicing. Leftovers the next day taste great too! You can make them the day before a party and then just warm them for 15-25 minutes in a low oven once the guests start arriving.

Stove Top

This is one of my only vegetarian meals when I make the mushroom or spinach variety, so it is a good addition to a cocktail party as a meatless appetizer or brunch option. It is also a great breakfast for Easter or Christmas morning (I can make it the night before instead of trying to actually cook during the chaos of opening gifts!)

Tips

*I cook 4 or 5 slices of bacon in the microwave until crisp, pat them with a paper towel and let them cool, then throw them into the Cuisinart mini-prep to chop them into small pieces. Much easier than cutting them!

**Microwave the spinach for half the time recommended on the box, then take the spinach out of the box and put it into a clean dish towel. Squeeze all the water out of the spinach and then add little pieces of spinach evenly around the pie. I usually use half the frozen box per quiche.

Best served with a nice salad (page 81) or to make it a hearty meal sometimes I serve with broccoli (page 78)

· · · · ·

Beef and Cheese Filled Gougere

INGREDIENTS LIST FOR FILLING

1 pound 90% lean ground beef (Or, if you like mushrooms then use less meat and add ½ cup mushrooms - baby bella work well)

1 small onion finely chopped

1 garlic clove small dice

1½ teaspoons chopped fresh thyme (Or ½ teaspoon dried thyme)

Freshly ground salt and pepper to taste

¾ cup (3 ounces) shredded part skim or whole milk mozzarella cheese

Preheat oven to 425 degrees. Grease a 10-inch round baking dish. Prepare filling by chopping onion, mincing the garlic clove, chopping fresh thyme (or measuring out dry), and if using mushrooms clean and slice them too.

If you didn't buy pre-shredded cheese then shred the mozzarella now and set aside. Prepare for the crust by putting the butter in a saucepan with the cold water. Pull out the eggs. Mix the flour in a bowl with the salt.

Filling: Brown the ground beef in a large skillet. Once it is just browned through drain some of the grease away. Add your onions, garlic, thyme and if desired mushrooms. Cook this until tender on med-low heat. While the flavored beef is cooking, you can start on the crust. Once the onions and mushrooms are tender (only takes 4-6 minutes), season with salt and pepper and turn off the burner.

Welcome to Fall!

I think of squash and pumpkin, cranberries and hearty soups, stews and goulash and most of all satisfying comfort food. The Fall spells chaos to parents of school age kids (we have 3 in grammar school); but, can be very comforting from a culinary point of few. It's goodbye salads and hello comfort food! This recipe bridges the transition from summer to Fall well - it's not too heavy, but very satisfying! I never make one Gougere - I always make two at a time. The second one becomes leftovers or can be frozen for a week or two. Now that I feed 5 hungry mouths at every meal, it goes too quickly to bother and freeze the second pie! This recipe makes one pie only, so I double it.

Beef and Cheese Filled Gougere

INGREDIENTS FOR THE CRUST

¼ cup butter

¾ cup cold water

¾ cup all-purpose flour

½ teaspoon salt

3 eggs

How to make the crust: Bring the butter and water to a boil and then turn off the heat once it starts to boil. Add the flour/salt mixture all at once and stir with a wooden spoon until the mixture is smooth and forms a ball. Move the flour mixture to a bowl and stir for a minute to cool it down before adding in the eggs. Add the eggs one at a time, beating well after each addition with a wooden spoon, so the egg is fully incorporated. Thinly spread dough onto bottom and up sides of your greased baking dish.

Fill crust with the ground beef mixture. Bake the gougere in preheated oven for 25 minutes (but check it at 20 minutes) - or until crust is puffed and golden brown. Sprinkle the meat with the shredded cheese and bake for another 5 minutes. Slice like a pizza and serve warm. Not bad as a leftover heated in the microwave the next day either.

Tips

Never run water over the mushrooms, use a damp clean dish towel and wipe them off instead, or clean off using a small mushroom brush.

Best served with steamed, sliced carrots tossed with butter and thyme or broccoli (page 78)

· · · · ·

Stove Top

While researching for my website, I found a very similar recipe to this crust recipe - "the classic Choux" (the addition of milk being the only difference, sometimes some sugar can also be added to choux as well). This is a savory choux, the sweet kind are used as vessels for cream puffs, éclairs and profiteroles. No wonder I love this crust so much!

Schnitzel

INGREDIENTS

6 thinly sliced boneless pork chops

Salt (enough to season both sides of each chop, and a pinch to sprinkle on the final schnitzel)

½ cup flour

Zest of one lemon

½ teaspoon pepper

1 egg

1 tablespoon milk

¾ cup fine bread crumbs (I use Progresso)

2 tablespoons canola oil (possibly need more for a second batch)

2 tablespoons unsalted butter

This is a purely German version of the lovely breaded meat! It is a great way to make something special from boneless pork chops that can be reasonably priced when on sale (picky eaters may even think it is chicken so just serve it without announcing what it is and watch them enjoy).

Tips

Remember, the pork is very thinly cut; be careful not to overcook it. Overcooked pork is tough and horrible. Cook in two batches Best served with ginger broccoli (page 78) and apple sauce (page 100)

• • • • •

The pork chops will be very thin already, but if they are uneven, use a meat mallet or bottom of a pan to flatten them to be the same thickness. Wrapping them in wax paper is helpful to avoid mess and sticking. Clean and trim the fat, then salt both sides.

Set up three bowls for breading the chops:

- Put the flour in the first shallow bowl (or pie tin), then mix in the lemon zest and a bit of pepper. (You can use lemon-pepper seasoning if you prefer.)

Dipping bowls

- In the second bowl, pour in the egg beaten with milk.

- In the third bowl, add bread crumbs.

Dip the pork into the flour and shake off the excess (all of it; if you don't get the extra flour off, the breading tends to fall off during cooking).

Next, dip the pork into the egg, then the bread crumbs, again shaking off the excess. Start the butter and oil heating over medium-high heat in a large nonstick pan while you finish dipping the chops and placing them on a plate.

When the oil/butter mixture is hot, carefully lay in the pork chops, one at a time. Do not overcrowd the pan; you will probably need to cook in two patches. Cook until browned on the first side, and then brown on the other side and remove to a plate. Add more butter and oil for the second batch if the pan is dry; they will cook better if there is enough butter and oil.

Taste for seasoning, and serve hot. Properly cooked, the meat will be white in the center. I usually grind a bit more salt on the hot schnitzels right before serving.

Perfect Scallops

INGREDIENTS

Small amount of canola oil (just enough to wipe a layer of it on the pan)

Large scallops

Fresh ground salt and pepper

SPECIAL EQUIPMENT

If possible, use a well-seasoned cast iron skillet; second choice would be a skillet that is not nonstick.

Put a layer of oil in the pan using a paper towel to wipe it around evenly. Heat the pan on high.

While the pan is warming up, rinse the scallops. Dry them well! I used a paper towel to thoroughly dry all sides of the scallops. Season both sides with salt and pepper. Put the scallops right into the hot pan.

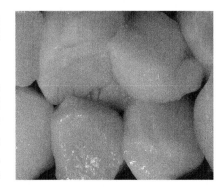

Do not turn the heat lower until all of the scallops are cooked and removed or they will leak water and stop caramelizing!

Leave space around each scallop, allowing it to get maximum heat.

Two minutes per side should be enough time to caramelize the scallops. They'll talk to you and let you know when it is time to turn. If they stick when you try to flip them with your tongs, they are not ready to turn! Serve with some lemon juice squeezed on top.

A great place to get cooking tips is right there in your local grocery store. One day, while at Whole Foods, I wanted to try to cook something from the sea. I prefer meat and chicken, but my husband and eldest son enjoy seafood and I want everyone happy. There were two women at the seafood counter who were an amazing help, and shared with me the trick to perfect scallops; I tried it, and it actually did work perfectly. Thanks ladies, for sharing your secrets. You rock!

Secrets

Scallops that have a yellowish, almost peach tone to them are the female scallops. They gain this color from having been surrounded by roe. The white scallops are the males (or females that have not yet matured). People don't always know this, but the "girls" tend to be tastier!

• • • • •

Turkey Chili

INGREDIENTS

1 tablespoon canola oil

1 tablespoon butter

1 large onion, diced

1 red bell pepper, small dice

2 garlic cloves, minced

1 teaspoon cumin

½ teaspoon dried oregano

2-3 tablespoons chili powder (it sounds like a lot, but this is chili after all!)

½ teaspoon cinnamon

1 tablespoon cocoa powder (this is not something that you will taste, but it will add a depth of flavor)

2 pounds ground turkey

2 tablespoons tomato paste

1 bottle dark beer (for depth of flavor, like the cocoa)

1 large can whole tomatoes

2 bay leaves

1 can small white beans

Salt and pepper to taste

Small chunk of sharp cheddar, grated for topping

Small red onion chopped finely, also for topping the chili

EQUIPMENT

Large Dutch oven or big stock pot

Peel and dice the onion and pepper and put aside in a small bowl. Dice the garlic and put into a really small bowl. Measure all of the dried spices and cocoa powder and reserve in another small bowl.

Put the canola oil and butter in the bottom of the Dutch oven or pot and cook over medium heat. Add the onion and pepper and a small pinch of salt. Cook until tender, 3-4 minutes. Add in the garlic and cook for another minute.

Add the ground turkey and break it into small chunks while browning the outside for 15 minutes or so. Sprinkle in the dried spice and cocoa powder mixture and the tomato paste. Add the whole tomatoes, bay leaves, white beans, 1 teaspoon salt and ½ teaspoon pepper.

Cook and stir over medium heat for another 45 minutes to 1 hour, until all of the flavors mix together and the meat is cooked through. You can also put into the oven at 325 degrees for an hour, but you still should open up the pot and stir every 10 or 15 minutes or so.

Best served either in bowls with a handful of grated sharp cheddar cheese and some chopped red onion on the top, or with warm multigrain or kaiser rolls like sloppy joes and health shakes (pages 111-115).

Stove Top

This chili tastes fantastic and is not too spicy. I can't handle too much spice, but if you can, then replace the red bell pepper with a hotter pepper of your choice and up the chili powder. You can also add some pinto beans; my kids just don't love beans so I stick to the small white ones that are better camouflaged. My husband is always amazed that this is made with ground turkey because it totally tastes like beef, but it is a leaner alternative.

Tips

Cut up the tomatoes either right in the can with a scissor, or in the pot; you can even break them up in your hands if you like to get properly "stuck in" as a cook! But we tried that, and the entire wall got splattered with red tomato juice, so I am back to the scissor.

If your chili is too bland that is an easy fix—just add more chili powder! But if it is too spicy for you or your family, fold in some sour cream to cut the spice and add a nice richness!

· · · · ·

Brandied Turkey Breast

INGREDIENTS

1 packet of 4 turkey cutlets

1 tablespoon butter

1 tablespoon olive oil

1 cup Wondra flour

1 teaspoon coriander

1 teaspoon salt

¼ teaspoon pepper

1 large orange (zest and juice)

¼ cup brandy (or chicken stock or white wine if preferred

This was the dilemma: I came home on a Friday night all set to go out or get a pizza, and there in the fridge staring me in the face was a packet of turkey cutlets with the sold-by date approaching fast. There go my plans right out the window! It was definitely too late for my favorite turkey cutlet recipe (breaded cheesy turkey), so I put together this little ditty. It's quick—and, tasty too!

Heat a nonstick pan on medium-high, add the butter and olive oil, and allow the butter to melt. Rinse and trim the turkey, then pat dry. Put the Wondra flour and the seasoning together in a bowl and whisk together. Put the seasoned flour in a gallon releasable bag, then put the turkey cutlets in the bag and move them around in the bag to coat.

Brown the cutlets in the pan on both sides, usually 3–4 minutes on the first side, then 2–3 minutes on the second. Add the zest, juice and brandy and cook for 5 minutes or until the alcohol is cooked out and the turkey is white through the center (cut into the thickest cutlet to check before serving).

Tips

This is great served with rice and peas and carrots (page 68)

· · · · ·

Creamy Potato Leek Soup

INGREDIENTS

2 quarts chicken stock, plus a bit (homemade, or I like unsalted Kitchen Basics and would use 2 large boxes and one small)

3 tablespoons unsalted butter

A drizzle of canola oil to prevent the butter burning

4 large leeks, cleaned and diced

2 large Spanish onions

1 teaspoon dried thyme

2 bay leaves

2 cloves garlic, chopped

1 teaspoon salt (plus a bit more, to taste)

½ teaspoon white pepper

4 russet potatoes, peeled and diced (medium dice, as you would use for mashed potatoes)

½ cup heavy cream

Melt the butter in a large Dutch oven or stockpot with a drizzle of oil. Add in the diced leeks, onions, thyme, bay leaves, garlic, salt and pepper and sauté until the vegetables are just getting tender, about 10–15 minutes. While the onions and leeks are heating, warm up the broth in a pot. After the vegetables are tender, add the broth to the onions and leeks and bring to a boil. Reduce to a simmer and cook for 30 minutes.

Add the potatoes and return to a boil, then reduce to a simmer again. If it looks a bit sparse, this is the time to add the extra 8 ounce container. Continue to cook for 20–25 minutes more, until the potatoes are tender. To check their tenderness, remove one from the soup and slowly push a fork through the middle; if it falls apart without much coaxing, consider them "tender".

Remove the bay leaves and add in the heavy cream. Use an immersion blender to cream the soup, or pour into a regular blender. Taste for seasoning and add more salt if needed.

Stove Top

I love soup all year round (in the same way that I love ice cream, no matter the weather!). This is a favorite of mine while eating out, so I thought I would try to make it at home. It was a huge success; you should give it a go. It looks more like pea soup than potato leek, but it's smooth and oniony, and the potatoes add heartiness.

One note about leeks: they have loads of dirt inside, so slice longwise twice, making four thinner sections so you can really clean the inside. Run them under cold water to make sure you get all the grit out.

Tips

Serve with caramelized onions or fried onions on top for some texture. (At a favorite steak restaurant I love, they add crunchy onions and a drizzle of aged balsamic on top, which is fantastic!) Serve with a nice loaf of warm crusty bread and you've made a hearty meal.

• • • • •

Tortellini Chicken Soup

INGREDIENTS

Package of chicken wings

Large split breast

8 carrots

8 celery stalks

2 medium onions

Fresh herbs (parsley, dill, thyme, rosemary or any combination) wrapped in cheese cloth

1 lemon

Large bag of tortellini for each portion of soup; you should have enough for one family meal, and you can buy a couple more bags when you thaw the leftover broth

Salt to taste

Rinse the chicken wings and breasts, then pat dry and place them in a large stock pot.

Add one carrot, the celery and the onions, very coarsely chopped, into a stock pot with the fresh herbs. Cover everything with water, putting enough to go a couple of inches higher than the chicken. Add 2 teaspoon of salt for a large pot of broth, and then taste as you go. Under-seasoned soup can taste like dirty dish water, but if it is too salty there is no turning back!

Bring to a boil over medium-high heat. Once boiling, squeeze in the lemon and skim the top (the lemon will clear away most of the residue that foams up to the top, but you can use a gravy ladle to get the rest).

Turn the heat down to medium-low once it reaches a boil, then simmer for 45 minutes to an hour, stirring occasionally. Meanwhile, dice the remaining carrot, celery and onion to small pieces.

Strain everything into another large pot with a colander or metal pasta strainer inserted over the second pot. Return the broth to the burner over medium-high heat. Add the diced veggies; bring to a boil and cook for 10 minutes.

While that's cooking, cool the breasts and then pull or slice off the white meat into small chunks; add those to the soup..

Once the veggies are soft, remove 3/4 of the soup to 2 or 3 containers to cool for freezing. Add to the remaining soup the tortellini and some fresh parsley (and/or dill) and boil for another 3 minutes (or whatever the tortellini directions state).

This is a must-try; the key is to make a huge pot of homemade broth with veggies and chicken and freeze most of it, keeping only enough for one meal in the refrigerator.

If you haven't noticed, my kids will eat anything that involves pasta. I guess that small piece of Sicilian ancestry is coming through, or maybe it is just a birthright of growing up in the northeastern US? My chicken soup gets lukewarm reviews (which is annoying since it takes an hour to make). But pour in a bag of tortellini and presto—it jumps up in the ratings and we get a complaint-free dinner for a change (although the pickiest of eaters will occasionally eat around all that other "stuff" and just eat the tortellinis - ugh!)

Tips

I add chicken wings to the broth, as I was told they have a lot of collagen, which adds flavor to the broth. You can reserve the wings after you strain the broth and strip the meat off to use in chicken salad, tacos, or a stir-fry.

· · · · ·

Veggies Even Picky Eaters will Love

When it comes to kids and veggies, it is rarely smooth sailing. I have worked for years to come up with simple flavor combinations that make fresh vegetables more appealing to the kids. To follow are my most successful recipes—they are fast, they are simple, and the flavors are straightforward. I was blessed with one kid who has a very adult pallet and enjoys all sorts of fruits, veggies, and spices as well, and I also have twins whose tastes are a bit more challenging so I have seen a glimpse into how difficult it can be to get healthy foods into the kids. Recently I have met many parents who really struggle with feeding fresh produce to their kids. I realize it can be a brutal uphill battle, and that the best recipes may not solve these issues, so I also want to share some thoughts.

Sometimes, veggies in their raw state go over best with children. Whenever you cook a new vegetable, keep a few raw and serve it both ways. Peppers, carrots, beans, broccoli, cauliflower can all be eaten raw and to a kid's pallet it may have a better taste. The crunch also is a selling point. If you know of a yogurt, mustard, or salad dressing they love, use it as a dip for raw fruits and vegetables. What if they love ketchup? Sounds gross to me, but if it gets them to eat veggies, I would pour it over them! If the kids "hate" peas, try including them into a soup, or cooking them in bacon fat (what doesn't taste better in bacon fat?) or add in some fresh mint from the garden or cook them with carrots and let them choose and pick out the carrots if they want, don't sweat it.

The best advice I can give when it comes to kids who don't eat vegetables is to never give up. I remember reading that kids need to try something over and again before you know they really don't like it. They can't stick their nose in the air once and then you give up. You may have many meals where the kids don't eat as well as you'd like, but you need to think long-term strategy to have them learn how to make healthy choices in the future. How I think you win is to keep the vegetables in front of the kids—have them grow them in the garden with you, go pumpkin pickin', teach them about how healthy they are and emphasize that we are all in charge of taking care of our own bodies. If you look at it as an education that will help them make better choices as adults, instead of a game where we win or they win depending on what they eat in a single meal, it will help you keep perspective.

When kids are little, include the veggies in soups, sauces, and stews and serve them alone. Expose them to as many different veggies as you can, even trick them sometimes. Be shameless! My mom used to call carrots "meat carrots" and eggplant parm "pizza meat." When the kids get to be school-age, bring them to the grocery store and make a game of trying new things. My eldest son and I used to choose a vegetable of the week (and some weeks a fruit of the week) together; we would find one he had never eaten, bring it home, look up recipes, and try it out. We found some really cool foods I hadn't even tried!

When the kids get to be in second or third grade, they realize that mommy and daddy can't make them do anything they really don't want to do. That's when the battles really begin. Recognizing this has helped me take a step back. I tell myself how important it is that they learn about healthy eating choices and taking care of themselves generally, but if they don't have a vegetable every day, that's OK.

I learned from my Aunt Joyce to offer two vegetable choices each dinner if possible. I took this a step further, and I also let them grab some raw baby carrots from the fridge if the cooked vegetables are not to their liking. Even my most challenging kid likes the raw baby carrots, so some weeks they eat quite a few of them. At this age, that is a success.

All Beans Are Not Created Equal!

BEANS FOUR WAYS

I was raised to believe that you had to eat green vegetables very frequently or you would evaporate or implode or be taken away by a spacecraft. Well, I'm not sure what would happen, but it wouldn't be good. This worry was somewhat squelched when I met a friend in high school who lived on hamburgers and Doritos and seemed whole and alive, but the paranoia still prevailed, if only in the back of my mind.

Seriously, because of my previous conditioning, there was a culinary cloud over my head when my kids would not eat beans or the dreaded peas. One evening, my eldest son, while out at a restaurant with the family, started eating his beans. Happily. I inquired, "Who are you and what have you done with my son?" He shared with me that these "restaurant beans" were good (unlike my humble version at home).

All the restaurants usually do is sauté their vegetables in oil, and that makes them desirable somehow. Well...I have olive oil, and a lot of other secrets up my sleeve! This is what I came up with:

Take two handfuls of fresh string beans and cook them briefly in a steamer basket for 3-4 minutes over boiling water, then follow one of the ideas on pages 64-66. Which direction I go depends on what is in my pantry, fridge, and garden at the time.

Beans are a vegetable we have had success growing in our Northeast climate in the summertime, but they can be tough to keep from becoming deer food. We have even better success with growing peppers, tomatoes and herbs- most of them make it to maturity without getting gobbled up by the local critters. Just lucky I guess.

Tips

My favorite beans are the thin French versions (haricot vert) but the big American ones are fine if they look nice and the skins are clean of brown lines and bruises. For the large string beans I cut not only the ends off but then cut them into shorter pieces with angular cuts (see photo). I have read that you only need to take off one end of the bean and the more tender pointy end can remain—most restaurants trim them in this way, but I take both ends off. Who needs 'em?

• • • • •

String Beans Almondine

INGREDIENTS

Two handfuls of fresh green beans, trimmed

¼ cup slivered almonds

1 tablespoon butter

Salt and pepper, to taste

Cook the beans in a steamer basket for 3-4 minutes over boiling water.

While the beans are steaming, heat 1 tablespoon of butter in a large skillet then throw in 1/4 cup slivered almonds and heat on medium. Don't let the nuts go dark brown or they will taste bitter.

I hit the nuts with 4 grinds of salt and 2 of pepper (enough to season the beans, as well). When the timer rings, dump the beans into the pan and sauté them with the almonds and butter for a couple of minutes. Check for seasoning, then serve.

Shallot Beans (or Garlic Beans)

INGREDIENTS

Two handfuls of fresh green beans, trimmed

1 shallot or 2 cloves of garlic diced

2 tablespoons olive oil

Salt and pepper, to taste

Either cut the shallot in half lengthwise and thinly sliced into half-moon strips or cut into small diced cubes like you would an onion—first long cuts down the half shallot, then across. If you are going the garlic route, crush the cloves, with the heal of your hand, peel them and chop finely.

Cook the beans in a steamer basket for 3-4 minutes over boiling water.

While the beans are steaming, heat 2 tablespoons of olive oil over medium-high heat in a large nonstick pan and cook the shallot for 3-4 minutes, until soft (or the garlic for 2 minutes not overcooking them, you don't want them brown).

Hit the shallots or garlic with 3 or 4 grinds of salt and 1 or 2 grinds of pepper right when they hit the oil; this will help pull the water from the shallots, and you need enough to also season the beans for either the shallot or garlic version. When the timer goes off, dump the beans into the oil mixture and sauté to doneness (another 2 or 3 minutes), check for seasoning, then serve.

Garden Tomatoes and Beans

When my husband's cherry tomato plant provides us with a handful of ripe cherry tomatoes, I prepare the garlic beans recipe on page 64, but add tomatoes. The proportion of beans to tomatoes depends on what you have ripe on the plant—I like to keep it at 50-50 if possible, but you can certainly add less if that's all you have!

INGREDIENTS

Two handfuls of fresh green beans, trimmed

2 cloves garlic

Cherry tomatoes, cleaned and halved

2 tablespoons olive oil

Salt and pepper, to taste

Fresh oregano, just a few leaves

Smash the garlic cloves with the heal of your hand, remove the peels, then chop into small pieces. You could use a garlic press, but then they turn into mush.

Warm up 2 tablespoon of olive oil in a large nonstick pan and cook the garlic for 2 minutes over medium-low heat (don't overcook or it will become bitter; if it turns dark brown dump it and start again).

Raise the heat to medium-high and add the tomatoes, salting generously (tomatoes love salt). Cook for 3 minutes. While the tomatoes are cooking, cook the beans in a steamer basket over boiling water for 3 minutes.

Add the steamed beans to the tomato mixture and cook for another 3–4 minutes and taste for seasoning. Chop the oregano roughly, sprinkle over the beans, and serve.

Lemon Bean Surprise

INGREDIENTS

Bunch of asparagus, trimmed

2 handfuls of fresh string beans

1 tablespoon butter

⅓ cup slivered almonds

Freshly crushed kosher salt and pepper, to taste

Zest of one lemon

Clean and cut the vegetables, then put them aside in a steamer basket. (For the asparagus, cut everything but the crowns into little short cylinders. Then cut the beans into very small segments similar in size to the asparagus.)

Boil water in a large steamer pot. While the water comes to a boil, heat the butter in a large skillet over medium-high. Once the skillet is hot, turn the flame down to medium, add the slivered almonds and some salt and pepper, and heat for 3–5 minutes.

As soon as the water in the pot comes to a boil, put the steamer basket in and let the vegetables steam for 4 minutes—any longer and they'll lose their vibrant green color. Once steamed, add the vegetables to the skillet and sauté them in the butter and almonds. Pour into a serving bowl and sprinkle with the lemon rind. Taste for seasoning and add more salt or pepper if need.

Tips

Even in a recipe where I am using butter as the fat, I drizzle a little canola or olive oil on the butter while it melts. This helps prevent the butter from burning.

- *Trick for trimming asparagus: Take the asparagus, even a few at a time, in your hand and snap them. Where it naturally breaks is exactly where it should, use the top half and throw the bottom away.*

- *My young chef son discovered that if you mixed rice into these vegetables it tasted great. It could even make for a nice vegetarian meal!*

- *The only way you can go wrong with this recipe is if you overcook the almonds, once they get dark they are bitter; or overcooking the beans to where they lose their bright color and nice texture. No one likes mushy, grey beans!*

• • • • •

One of my children likes asparagus and the other two do not, and neither does my husband! So what am I supposed to do when I buy that big bunch of asparagus and only two of us will eat them? I decided today to try a new way to "market" the asparagus to the family. I cut just the bottoms of the asparagus up until the crown and mixed it in with string beans and added some flavorings that go over well with everyone in the family. My husband took a spoon full and thought it was all beans—it worked!

Give Peas a Chance!

PEAS THREE WAYS

Microwaved frozen vegetables may be the fastest veggie to make on a busy weekday night, but they are usually not the tastiest or healthiest, with one exception. Frozen sweet baby peas are tasty, and work better than the fresh version for a quick midweek meal. Unfortunately, half of my family dislikes them at the moment (the kids tend to go in picky cycles, and have been fighting peas for a couple of years; it has been a long and bitter battle that I hope will end soon). I have been inspired to win this battle by bumping up the flavor of the peas, and here are some of my favorite ways:

Gourmet Peas

INGREDIENTS

2 slices bacon

1 shallot, diced

Package of frozen peas

Salt and pepper, to taste

Put the bacon in the freezer for 20 minutes, then remove, and cut into small pieces. Fry in a skillet until crispy.

Remove the bacon and add the diced shallot. Salt the shallot and cook for 3 minutes while microwaving the frozen peas. Once the shallots are soft, add the almost cooked peas (if the package says cooking time is 6 minutes, only cook them for 5 minutes) to the pan with the drippings and shallots and put the bacon back in. (If there is too much bacon grease, just dump some out.)

Stir the ingredients over medium heat for a minute or two, grind a bit of pepper and salt over them, and serve. This has a fantastic sweetness from the peas and onions, as well as the little surprise of the salty meatiness from the bacon.

I tried to replicate a pea dish I had at a restaurant and came pretty darn close with this recipe.
Peas and pork seem to be good friends; I can remember my mom making homemade pea soup with that big ham swimming in the thick green liquid.

Peas and Carrots

INGREDIENTS

4 carrots

Package of frozen baby peas with no sauce

Butter, salt, and pepper, to taste

Tips

Peas Inside: Most of my one-dish meals do really well with the addition of a handful of frozen baby peas. Chicken pot pie, beef stew, soups, risotto (page 17), and pasta dishes (page 33) all taste better with some peas (although my kids may not agree). Peas cook very quickly, so add them near the end of the cooking time almost as you would a fresh herb but giving them 5–10 minutes within the sauce or soup so they are cooked all the way through.

· · · · ·

Use a vegetable steamer to cook four carrots, peeled and diced into whatever shape or size you like, until they are halfway cooked (I cooked the carrots in the picture by steaming them for 3 minutes before adding the baby peas).

Pour the frozen baby peas into the carrots and steam for 4–5 minutes according to the package instructions. Hit it with a tablespoon of butter and freshly ground salt and pepper, stir, and serve hot.

When my kids eat this they pick out the carrots, but are bound to get a pea in there once in a while. I wish they would stop squirming about peas already, they are so sweet!

Peas and Barley

INGREDIENTS

½ cup barley

1 ½ cup water or stock

Half a bag of baby sweet peas (7 ounces)

1 tablespoon butter (or more if you are skipping the cheese topping)

Salt and pepper, to taste

¼ cup Parmesan reggiano, shredded to top the dish (optional)

Cook the barley per the directions on the bag, using stock if you have it instead of water to give it more flavor. Four minutes before the barley is completely cooked, add the frozen baby peas. Stir in the butter and season with salt and pepper. Taste for seasoning and adjust. Top the final product with Parmesan reggiano cheese for an extra boost of flavor.

Tip

Great served with some turkey cutlets (page 55), or marinated pork tenderloin (page 11).

Necessity is the mother of invention as they say, and I had a small amount of barley leftover from my beef barley soup that I didn't know what to do with. I just knew I didn't want to waste such a versatile ingredient. Barley tastes nutty, but also a bit like pasta too, and it is so healthy as a whole grain while having a pleasing taste that it can offer an easy way to get some nutrition into the kids. I invented this dish because I had the barley and I love baby peas, and had seen them paired in the past before. It tasted pretty good, and was so quick and easy as a side dish! Healthy….quick…. easy, the three most important adjectives for a busy home kitchen!

Glazed Carrots

INGREDIENTS

4 large carrots, cleaned and peeled

2 tablespoon unsalted butter

Zest and juice of one large orange

1 tablespoon honey

¼ to ½ cup water or chicken stock

Salt and pepper, to taste

These are my twins' favorite—and I think they are pretty tasty, as well! Carrots are already sweet, so the addition of a little honey and orange juice brings them to the next level of delicious.

Cut your carrots on a bias and start to melt your butter over medium-high heat in a pan or soup pot. Add the carrots, orange zest, orange juice, honey and about 1/4 cup water or chicken stock to the melted butter.

Heat while stirring frequently for 10 minutes. Don't let the pan get completely dry;. add a bit of water or stock if needed. You want most of the liquid to evaporate as the carrots glaze—just be careful they don't burn.

Once the carrots are tender and most of the liquid is gone, they can be seasoned with salt and pepper and served immediately.

Tips

Great with pork tenderloin skewers (page 11) and peas with barley (page 69).

· · · · ·

VEGGIES | Carrots Two Ways **71**

French Carrots

INGREDIENTS

1 bag of baby carrots (around a pound), plus another handful if you have extra

1 egg

2 tablespoons olive oil

1 tablespoon Dijon mustard (I used

Grey Poupon; remember those old commercials with the limo? I may be showing my age!)

1 tablespoon white wine vinegar

Zest from half of a lemon

½ teaspoon salt

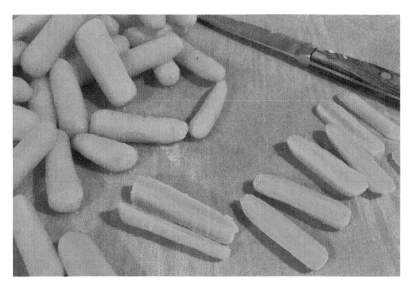

Cook the carrots for 15 minutes in a steamer basket. While they cook, combine all of the remaining ingredients into a bowl and whisk.

Once the carrots are cooked, spray them with cool water so they can be handled. Pat dry with a clean dish cloth then slice lengthwise into thin strips.

Now here is the tricky part: Get a cold nonstick pan and pour in the sauce and the carrots. Put the flame very low and warm the carrots and sauce through for 10 minutes while stirring the whole time. Viola—French carrots to impress your family!

Tip

The first time I tried to make this, I placed the cooked carrots and the sauce into a pan that was already hot—big mistake! The sauce has an egg in it, so it almost instantaneously turned to scrambled eggs, all lumpy and gross. If you follow these instructions exactly, you will have an elegant side dish in about 15 active minutes, 35 minutes start to finish.

• • • • •

Carrots and broccoli are the two vegetables that all three kids eat, so when I can find a new way to serve them I jump on it. Reading through the very popular Italian cookbook The Silver Spoon I learned about making carrots with "French sauce" (ironic, no?). The Silver Spoon has been around for decades, and I have been told it is the best-selling cookbook there for over 50 years, and is given to just about every newly married couple. I followed that recipe once with lukewarm results, then tried again tweaking it, adding in lemon rind and a bit more salt. Once I figured out how best to warm the final concoction, it worked really well!

Would taste great with grilled burgers (page 3) and homemade French fries (page 90)

Fresh and Zingy Mixed Veggies

INGREDIENTS

Stick of butter (softened)

1 tablespoon Dijon or grainy mustard

1 tablespoon chopped fresh chives

Zest of one lemon, grated

Freshly ground salt, pepper, and nutmeg, to taste (I use 1 teaspoon or so of each)

1 head of cauliflower

1 portion of broccoli (usually 3 heads tied together)

4 carrots peeled and sliced in diagonal chunks

Handful of snow peas (optional)

Place the softened butter into a medium mixing bowl. Add the mustard, chopped chives, lemon zest, salt, pepper, and nutmeg and mix thoroughly.

Put a steamer basket in a pot that has a lid and heat a few inches of water in it.. Steam the cauliflower and large carrot chunks for 3 minutes. Then add the broccoli and snow peas (if using) and steam for another 3 minutes. Turn off the flame, take the basket of vegetables out of the pot, remove the water, and pour the vegetables into the hot, empty pot.

Add the flavored butter and stir it around the hot vegetables so that it coats them all evenly. If you are not serving immediately, you need to cool off the vegetables by placing them into a bowl over an ice bath. When they're cool, put them into a microwaveable baking dish in the refrigerator to chill until you need them. Microwave the dish for 3 minutes and check if they are warm; if not, keep heating in one-minute intervals until they are warm. Pour them out into your serving dish and enjoy!

> I use this recipe for family occasions all the time because everyone seems to love the flavor of the sauce; the lemon and chives are refreshing and the mustard adds a nice depth and richness. Its light, refreshing flavor is very nice in the springtime. It's great for entertaining since, some people like just cauliflower, others only carrots, and everyone can just pick out their favorites. It's also highly adaptable—use whatever proportions you like.

Steamed zucchini mixed veggies

INGREDIENTS

1 Green zucchini

1 Yellow zucchini

3 large carrots

1 tablespoon butter

Salt and pepper to taste

Tip

If your kids like cheese, you can top with some grated Parmesan

• • • • •

Clean and peel carrots and clean the zucchinis while you heat water in the bottom of a steamer pot. Cut the zucchinis and carrot into very thin matchstick shapes, all the same size or just buy pre-cut. Steam the veggies until tender, only will take 2-3 minutes, just taste one to check if they are tender enough for your taste. Toss the veggies in large bowl with the butter and seasoning while still hot and serve right away.

Mom's Stuffed Artichokes

INGREDIENTS

1 container of anchovies in oil

Salt

4 artichokes

Clean the artichokes under cold water. Use a knife to cut the top of the artichokes and the bottoms so they can sit flat in the pot. Use a scissor to snip the pointed tops of the outer leaves. Use a deep pot with a lid; fill with enough water to go partially up the side of the artichoke. Salt the artichoke on the outside all over, and add a few shakes of salt to the water in the pot as well. Use about 3 or 4 anchovies per artichoke, and pull them in half. Stuff each anchovy half in between the artichoke leaves, some on the outer leaves and some on the inner leaves.

Lay the artichokes in the bottom of the pot with water and heat the water on high until it boils. Once it boils, put the heat down to medium-high and put a lid on the pot so the steam cookes the artichokes. Check them every so often, make sure the water does not boil away, that happened to me once and I burnt my pot! Awful!

After about 25 minutes try to pull an outer leaf, and if it easily comes off the artichokes are fully cooked. If not, leave them for more steaming and check on them every 5 minutes until complete. Serve hot as an appetizer, that's the way we do it in our family. It would be weird as a side dish, it takes a while to eat these so the rest of the dinner would go cold as you eat leaf by leaf.

Once you have eaten all of the leaves, you will see a hairy looking "choke". Use your knife to cut out the choke as it is inedible, but don't toss that meaty flavorful heart at the bottom. The heart is the prize, it tastes fantastic! The heart keeps me going leaf by leaf through the artichoke; just the anticipation of that yumminess makes the effort worthwhile.

Serve with a big drizzle of the now flavored water over the artichoke and make sure there is a paring knife handy handy for getting to the heart.

Variation: Aunt Joyce used to stuff her artichokes with breadcrumbs and garlic, I haven't tried that but I remember as a kid it tasted great!

During the edit of this book I discovered that my Mom learned this method of preparing artichokes from her paternal Sicilian grandma, Serafina. This dish is a childhood favorite of mine, and now it means even more to me, as I realize my kids are at least the 5th generation to enjoy them! I don't even like fish, but adding in the anchovies creates a salty kick that this vegetable needs.

Tips

Buy artichokes when they are in season, make sure that you choose the type that come to a point at the top, I have cooked the ones that are more of a round shape and they were tough.

Rinse off the oil from the anchovies if you'd like, but Mom told me to keep them the way they are, AND to drip some oil onto the tops of the artichokes – those are the little Mom secrets that add flavor.

When eating the thick outer leaves scrape the tasty inside, but the thin inner leaves can be eaten almost whole, but the pointy top.

* * * * *

Ginger Broccoli

INGREDIENTS

1 large head of organic broccoli (the one with three stalks tied together), or 2 large crowns

Three swirls of olive oil (approximately 1 tablespoon)

2 inches of fresh ginger, finely diced

2 cloves of garlic, finely diced

Salt and pepper, to taste

The one vegetable that all three kids will eat is broccoli, but only if it is prepared as outlined below. This is a "by kids for kids" recipe because it was the first dish my eldest son could make all by himself!

Clean and cut the broccoli florets while you start water boiling in the bottom of a double boiler. (The water only needs to be 2–3 inches up the side of the pot.) Heat the broccoli for 3–4 minutes while you warm the olive oil in the pan with the garlic and ginger. Dump the still steaming broccoli into the pan and coat with the oil, garlic, and ginger while hitting it with some freshly ground salt and pepper, to taste.

If not serving right away, I stick it in the freezer for 10 minutes to cool it down so it doesn't overcook, then I put it in the refrigerator until we need it.

Tips

The easiest way I've found to get the skin off of a garlic clove is to smash it with the heel of my hand then the skin peels right off.

Broccoli can easily overcook and just fall apart, so better to undercook then overcook. There is no way back from overcooked broccoli, while under cooked broccoli has more vitamins.

From the first time I allowed my kids to use a knife or peeler (8-years-old in the case of my eldest, a bit younger for my twins since they are always playing catch-up) I have them wear a knife glove on their opposing hand to protect it if they slip. No cuts yet, so it is working out well!

· · · · ·

Garlic Sautéed Spinach

INGREDIENTS

2 tablespoons extra virgin olive oil

2 cloves garlic, diced

1 bag fresh spinach leaves

Freshly ground salt and lemon pepper, to taste

¼ teaspoon freshly ground nutmeg

There is nothing quicker and healthier than wilting some fresh spinach as a side dish. To make it tastier, just hit it with garlic and seasoning. The first time you see a big bag of fresh spinach (or any leafy green) wilt down in a hot pan, the transformation is pretty cool to witness—it just shrinks down so quickly. Show your kids this trick, and maybe it will be intriguing enough for them to eat their spinach! Confession: It doesn't always work in my house, but Dad and I enjoy this even when the kids don't.

Pour a few drizzles of olive oil into a pan over medium-high heat. Crush two cloves of garlic into the warming oil and cook for 1 minute. Add the spinach all at once. Use prongs to keep turning the fresh spinach around to coat it with the olive oil, and to mix the garlic and get the spinach wilting; this will take only 90 seconds.

Right before you serve the spinach, season with salt, pepper and nutmeg. A bag of spinach will wilt down to such a small amount as to only feed two or three spinach lovers, so you might need two bags to feed your family (if you are one of the fortunate few who can get the kids to eat spinach).

Getting Kids to Eat Salads

My kids don't love salad, but I don't give up easily. Clearly you can teach them to "eat their salad" with less drama if you include their favorite ingredients only, instead of battling them to eat things they are at war against. Stick to what they like, and maybe try one new thing at a time.

There are so many healthy salad toppings available at the grocery store these days including ingredients like sunflower seeds, nuts, even dried cranberries. These toppers can help make a salad more desirable for our picky kids.

Lettuce Tips

For Romaine lettuce you rinse it and then cut strips with a knife. For Iceberg break it apart in your hands, and for the bags that say they are triple washed, I still would rinse them anyway, who knows. I tend to avoid the bagged lettuce mixes and the pre-cut vegetables, it all seems very dried out and shriveled up to me. I would rather get it fresh and cut it myself!

· · · · ·

Sweetness Helps

I make a virtually all fruit salad on a bed of romaine or iceberg lettuce and add baby carrots for the pickiest eaters. The more daring of the lot, can handle some orange or yellow peppers and celery as well. I always use the celery leaves mixed with the lettuce, and when I it on hand, I add fresh spinach leaves or a couple of basil leaves, as long as there are sweet fruits included there is a greater chance they will eat the other ingredients.

Some favorite fruits we add to our salads: Fuji apples and green grapes. Segments of Clementine oranges go well with Vidalia onion dressing. Strawberries just add such a pop of color!

Getting Kids to Eat Salads

Add a bit of Crunch and Texture

Sometimes I put walnuts or almonds on top, or I shave Parmesan cheese over the salads. Chopped pecans, walnuts, or slivered almonds make salads more kid friendly and add protein. A little crunch is good. Whatever works to start good habits, that's my motto!

Use Freshest Local Ingredients Possible!

Take the kids to a local farmer's market to pick local ingredients, or better yet, grow them yourself.

It is October, and we are still pulling cherry tomatoes off of the plant in our backyard and building salads around them (as well as using them to make quick pasta/pizza sauces).

The Dressing Dilemma

Sometimes my kids like a little ranch or Italian dressing, but the store bought dressings are full of sugar (in whatever sinister form). Sometimes we just serve our salads 'naked' or with a squeeze of lemon, but here are two ideas that may work:

Quick Russian Dressing: My Mom used to take ketchup and mayo (2 parts mayo to 1 part ketchup) and mix in some sliced green olives and stir - ta da! Russian dressing!

Light Summer Dressing: You can also drizzle some olive oil, a squeeze of lemon juice and shake some salt and pepper into a clean baby food jar and shake it up to make a quick dressing. My family didn't like it plain though, so also add in a strong flavor the kids like, mustard may work or some grated parmesan cheese, then they might go for it. It is worth trying different flavor combinations for a homemade dressing, to avoid the sugar and preservatives found in store bought dressings, but still add the right flavors to dress-up this healthy side dish.

Grilled Eggplant

INGREDIENTS

1 large eggplant

1 lemon

Freshly ground salt and pepper

1 tablespoon olive oil

1 teaspoon fresh oregano leaves

The perfect quick summer veggie. Eggplant can be meaty and substantial served simply with some fresh herbs, olive oil and lemon. Some people will salt the slices of eggplant and lay them in a colander or on paper towels to remove any bitterness, then rinse them off and proceed with their recipe. I haven't found this step necessary, so I skip it.

Tip

This is great with marinated chicken or pork (page 9).

. . . . .

Peel the eggplant and slice into one-inch rounds. Squeeze the lemon juice on both sides, hit both sides with a bit of olive oil, then dust with freshly ground salt and pepper. Grill on both sides for 4–5 minutes or until nice grill marks are made and the eggplant is heated through. Before serving, drizzle with olive oil, sprinkle on the fresh oregano leaves, and add a bit more salt.

Variation: You can treat the large portabello mushrooms similarly, I would just use fresh thyme leaves to top. This is a good "meaty" vegetable alternative for actual barbecued meat if you are cutting down.

Grilled Corn on the Cob

INGREDIENTS

1 fresh corn on the cob per person

Spray olive oil

Up to 1 tablespoon of butter per ear of corn (softened)

Salt and pepper

Aluminum wrap

This one is incredibly easy to make and tastier than boiled corn as the barbecuing gives the flavor more layers. Corn is a blank canvas so any favorite dry spice could be sprinkled on the corn before grilling, be adventurous. Great side dish to make during a kitchen reno when all you have is the grill.

Husk the corn in the store if possible. Corn should be husked the day you are cooking it (sometimes a large cardboard box is provided by the store so you can get the job done). It is messy to husk corn but you don't want to buy corn out of the husk since it will be dry and less fresh. An alternative is to husk the corn in your backyard and put the skin and silt in a paper bag.

Rinse the corn and dry it. For each corn take enough aluminum foil to wrap the corn. Spray the inside of the aluminum foil with the olive oil so the corn doesn't stick to the wrap. For flavor, spread some butter on the corn and hit each corn with salt and pepper to your taste.

Place your wrapped corn on a medium hot barbecue grill and cook for 15-20 minutes, turning every 5 minutes. You will know it is cooked when a fork pushed into the kernels prove that they are tender.

Great served with barbecued hamburgers and sausage (page 7) and nice fresh string bean side dish (page 63)

Tip

The yellow and white corn available fresh from local farms in the summertime in my area is the sweetest. If corn is out of season, just stick with the frozen kernel corn.

- - - - -

Campfire Potatoes

INGREDIENTS

3–5 russet potatoes

1 large yellow onion

Stick of butter, softened a bit
(you may not need it all, but have
it just in case)

Freshly ground salt and pepper

Heavy-duty aluminum foil

I add these to the menu
whenever we have an
extra 15 minutes while
barbecuing. They
taste great and aren't
that difficult. If you
are having guests just
make a couple of sacks
of them and you are
good to go!

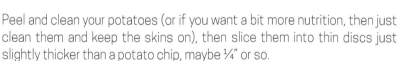

Tip

*If you still have leftover potatoes,
make a second pouch. If you only
have two layers of potatoes they will
brown well.*

· · · · ·

Peel and clean your potatoes (or if you want a bit more nutrition, then just clean them and keep the skins on), then slice them into thin discs just slightly thicker than a potato chip, maybe ¼" or so.

Peel and clean the onion—cut it first in half the long way and then put each half flat side down and slice ½" slices, letting the layers fall apart.

Place the potatoes in one bowl and the onion pieces in another and have your stick of butter, salt and pepper handy .

Lay out a piece of heavy duty aluminum foil (about 3½ feet long) on the counter. Fold over one foot of foil, then put dabs of butter all over the area where the potatoes will be placed. Then, start layering your ingredients in the center of the doubled foil—a layer of potatoes, then a layer of onions,

Campfire Potatoes

then season with salt and pepper. Repeat once more then end with a layer of butter so the top foil won't stick and the potatoes brown. Leave enough room on the bottom and side to seal the pouch. Season with freshly ground salt and pepper.

Fold the foil over the potatoes and seal the three sides tightly so nothing will escape. Cook on a preheated charcoal or gas grill about 15–20 minutes per side, checking to see if the potatoes have browned.

Finished potatoes should be tender. Not all of them will brown, but most of them should be browned before you consider them done. I'm afraid I can't tell you how delicious these are, so you'll just have to try for yourself!

Patriotic Potatoes

INGREDIENTS

Bag of small potatoes (mixed red, yellow, and purple)

Salt for the water

2 tablespoons olive oil

1 small white onion (or 2 shallots), thinly sliced

2 tablespoons butter

Freshly ground salt and pepper, to taste

2 tablespoons fresh herbs*

Zest of one lemon (optional)

My eldest son invented this recipe. One day at the grocery store he noticed that you could buy potatoes in three colors, so we bought a bag of them and came up with a recipe for them together. We thought the skins were close enough to red, white, and blue to be pretty patriotic. It being summer, our garden had lots of fresh herbs ready to incorporate into our new dish, so it was a no-brainer.

*I use equal parts lemon thyme and parsley with a bit of rosemary for good measure, but regular thyme or fresh oregano would be good, too. A dried mix like Herbes de Provence also works.

Clean the potatoes (but don't peel them, or you lose the nutrition and the skin color). Cut the small or medium sized potatoes in half, and the larger potatoes in quarters. More surface area will allow for more caramelization and crunchy bits.

Put the potatoes in cold water in a large pot (using the pasta insert if you have a steamer pot) for 15 minutes. Salt the water, then place the pot over high heat . Keep the lid on the pot until it comes to a boil, then remove the lid and let it boil for 5 minutes. Check the potatoes for doneness; they just need to be a bit soft, but still have a bite to them.

Drain the potatoes, then put them in a large bowl. Drizzle half the olive oil over them then, while the potatoes are still hot, add salt and pepper, to taste, and the zest. Toss well.

Heat a large skillet and add the other half olive oil to the pan. Once it is hot, add the onions and salt them; cook for 3–4 minutes until translucent. Then throw in the potatoes and the butter. Cook until the potatoes are brown. This takes a bit of time, so don't stir them too often or they won't brown properly. Once most potatoes are browned they are ready and can be served immediately. Sprinkle on the fresh herbs right before serving and toss them around.

Nice served with grilled marinated meat (pages 9-11) or turkey cutlets (page 55).

Tip

This recipe can also be done with any small potatoes, or with quartered yukon gold potatoes, you will just not get the brilliant vibrant colors, but the flavors will be spot on.

• • • • •

Homemade French Fries

INGREDIENTS

2 very large russet potatoes, or 3 medium

Canola oil (enough for a thick layer in your pan)

Freshly ground salt and pepper, to taste

This is a quick way I make French fries at home without a deep fryer. (I had one once but it was pretty cumbersome to use, wash, and even just to store so I adapted.) When you cut the potatoes, keep the skins on; most of the nutrition hides between the skin and flesh, and the skin adds fiber.

Scrub your potatoes under cool water. Slice them into wedges larger than the shoestring fries of fast food, but smaller than oven fries. I have cut them super thin before, and they aren't as good.

Soak in cold water for 10 or 15 minutes to draw out some of the starch. Put the fries on paper towels and microwave on high for 2 minutes.

Heat the canola in the pan over medium-high until it sizzles when you drop some water in, or dip a fry in and see if it sizzles. If it does, the oil is ready (always be careful around the sizzling oil, and keep the kids away).

Dry off any moist fries and drop them gently into the oil. Do no overcrowd the pan; it's better to do two batches and let them have room to cook

Tricks

Season with your favorite dried spices, dried herbs. Throw on some Parmesan cheese and truffle oil to be a fancy pants, or melt mozzarella on them and dip into gravy as a reminder of drunken nights in college when you hit the diner after the bar (remember those diner runs?) Potatoes are a blank canvass, the sky's the limit!

· · · · ·

properly. Heat the fries for a couple of minutes, using tongs to turn them over when they're brown on the bottom. Remove them from the oil when they're brown on both sides.

Shake off the oil in a brown paper bag and season the fries while hot. Lay them on a paper towel to continue soaking up any residual oil. Serve immediately!

These are nice to serve with a big grilled steak (page 5) and a quick sautéed spinach (page 79) or fresh crisp salad (page 81).

Tip

This version can be soggy if you don't keep the oil hot enough; remember to soak the fries in water first but make sure they're dry before you add them to the oil.

· · · · ·

Fast Potatoes (Ten-Minutes)

INGREDIENTS

2 shallots, diced

1 package fresh gnocchi

2 tablespoons butter

Splash of canola oil

Salt and pepper, to taste

1 teaspoon fresh lemon thyme (no stems)

1 teaspoon fresh finely chopped rosemary

I once saw a celebrity chef cook gnocchi (generally a potato-filled pasta served with sauce) in butter until they browned and turned into tiny versions of roasted potatoes. That gave me the inspiration for this super fast side dish! You should be able to find fresh gnocchi in the refrigerated section with the other fresh pasta and pierogies.

Heat butter and oil in a large skillet over medium-high heat. Once the pan is hot, add the shallots.

Salt the shallots and cook for 2 minutes. Add the gnocchi and brown both sides. Season with salt and pepper, then sprinkle with the fresh herbs right before you serve.

Even Faster Potatoes (Five-Minutes)

This is the pinnacle of home-made "fast food" when you are really crunched for time. I am not promising health food here, just speed (although I do buy the all-natural pierogies).

In the refrigerated section of the grocery store you will find flavored pierogies next to the fresh pasta. I like to buy the onion pierogies, and cook them in a skillet coated with canola oil. Once they are brown on both sides, I shake them in a paper bag with salt and pepper to get the grease off of them, and they are ready to serve.

These fried pierogis remind me of when I went to school in Pennsylvania, and on my ride home I would go through the drive through at Yocco's, the Hot Dog King. Nutrition was not high on the priority list in college. I love the hot crispy outside and smooth steamy mashed potato in the middle.

Typically pierogis are boiled in water or sautéed in butter and onions, I just decided to fry them in Canola oil one day. The kids loved them and it took me no time at all, so we now make these often (and just pair them with a healthy veggie and lean protein).

During the school year, I typically cook in mass quantities on Sunday, which allows for leftovers Monday through Wednesday. Thursday is the wild card day. In addition to having no leftovers left over, I have two kids in piano lessons from 6:00-7:00, and an 8:30 bedtime for all three kids. I literally have to rush home from work and get some food together, feed the twins, and arrive at the piano lesson by 6:00 or they are starving at piano. It's a bit crazy, so my solution is to do pierogies, cut some fruit, and make a quick vegetable like fresh spinach sautéed in garlic and olive oil or frozen peas and some kind of quick protein.

Fruits and Fruit Desserts

It's no secret that kids love sweet treats; start early, when they're toddlers, to serve fruit as the dessert after dinner. Serve fruit as a staple part of breakfast too, and you will be able to get some extra vitamins into the whole family's diet. I talk to a lot of moms who have issues with picky eaters, and fruit seems to pose as much of a challenge as vegetables do, so here are some of my secrets.

Put as many different types of fruits in front of your kids as possible. Do not give up; they may hate bananas now but love them in a year. If they hate them and never look back, then bake with them (pages 141-143) or include them into healthy shakes (pages 111-115). That has worked really well in my house, where two of three kids haven't eaten bananas in years. Oddly enough, they both also like banana chips and will eat banana bread, as well. I guess it has more to do with the texture than the flavor, although they sometimes complain if I put too much banana into the health shake so I have to be creative and hide it with a strong fruit juice like orange or pineapple.

My kids all love yogurt, so we tend to start with yogurt and build parfaits (page 106) with fruits and crunchy ingredients; that helps the fruit go down. All my kids love whipped cream (page 139), so putting some berries with whipped cream can make the difference, or taking tart strawberries or a half of a pink grapefruit and just adding a sprinkle of sugar on top.

With some fruit, it may be better to "hide" them in a crowd of fruits; try a fruit cup (page 96) or a creamy fruit cup (page 96). It may help to prepare it in a new way, like grilling a pineapple (page109), cooking it into a sauce (page 108), or blitzing it with some sugar into a topping for ice cream (page 108). The possibilities are endless, so never give up! Real ingredients pump up the flavor as well as the health in our meals and desserts.

We also go on a family adventure each September to an orchard for apple picking, which gives them a chance to see how the food grows, pick exactly which types to try, and then to try all different levels of sweetness and tartness. It is always helpful to bring kids to learn where the food comes from, be it farms, farmer's markets, or even having them help you grow strawberries or fruit trees in your yard. There is something very special about picking your own food; you can't go out on a nice sunny day for a car trip to see Oreo trees or run through fields of Kit Kats! Real food that comes from the earth is something kids these days don't always connect to, so it is our job to educate them on the natural beauty and flavor of fresh fruits.

Fresh Fruit Cup

Talk about easy! Every weekend in the summer I get fresh, ripe produce and just cut it up small and toss it together. I squeeze half of an orange over all the cut fruit for a little extra zing and to keep the apple flesh white. I also sprinkle in a little sugar for some surprise sweetness in case any of the fruit is not quite ripe. This is not just a summertime treat, though; I also serve a fruit cup every Thanksgiving at the beginning of the meal, and all year round depending on what fruits are in season or available. It's always fantastic and lasts a couple of days in the fridge.

Here's a typical recipe I use, but any colorful fruit that your family loves, cubed in small chunks, will work just as well.

INGREDIENTS

Handful of green and purple grapes (sliced in half for the little kiddies)

3 Fuji apples cut in small cubes

Handful of blueberries

Firm banana, sliced

Cut melon, very ripe (I usually use pineapple, cantaloupe or watermelon)

1 orange (one half for squeezing over the salad and the other half cut up with the rest of the fruit)

1 teaspoon sugar

Sliced strawberries

Handful of raspberries

1-2 kiwis, sliced

Tips

I have found that pears don't hold up well, so I tend not to use them. I'll also leave out the bananas if they are too ripe— they tend to get mushy, quick!

· · · · ·

Stir together the grapes, cubed apples, blueberries, banana slices, melon, orange slices and sugar. Squeeze the half orange over the top, then sprinkle with the sugar. Add raspberries and sliced strawberries (they're just too delicate to mix in with the sugar and orange), then top with kiwi slices.

Creamy Fruit Cup

To shake things up, I recently added in some "dressing" and as is usually the case, some of my family loved it, others did not (usually things get mixed reviews in my house). For those feeling adventurous, it's a must try.

INGREDIENTS

Whisk together:

½ a cup of Greek yogurt

¼ cup sour cream

Splash of vanilla extract

2 shakes of cinnamon

Honey, to taste (I use about 1 teaspoon)

Stir it into the fruit cup and hope your children have an open mind!

Berry Salad

I recommend adding whipped cream (page 139) to this (homemade or store-bought will do), or pouring the berries over small shortcakes or slices of grilled pound cake—whatever it takes to get your picky eaters to take in those antioxidants! This salad can be the base for a mixed berry crumble (page 98) as well.

Another no brainer! Just cut up about eight strawberries and add to a bowl with a half cup each blueberries, blackberries and raspberries. Squeeze half an orange over the berries and add six fresh mint leaves, rolled up and sliced into thin ribbons (chiffonade, if you want to get fancy). Stir to combine. Taste the salad; if it's too tart, add a teaspoon of sugar and mix well.

SECRET

Oranges! Everything goes better with a bit of orange zest and/or juice. You will see I have recipes that include orange from turkey breasts (page 55) to chocolate cookies (page 125) to marinades (page 9)!

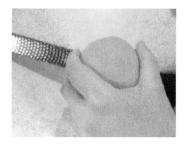

Trick

Mint grows like a crazy weed with a horizontal root system, so even if you plant only one mint plant you can have tons of mint all summer. Seriously worth the investment (plant it in a pot if you don't want to have to cut it back all the time as it takes over the garden). Great for cooking, baking and adding to tea.

• • • • •

Triple Berry Crumble

INGREDIENTS

5 cups berries (I use mostly blueberries, then a half pint of raspberries and a half pint of blackberries)

Zest and juice of 2 lemons

½ cup sugar

¼ cup all-purpose flour

½ teaspoon cinnamon

(For the topping)

¾ cup flour

¼ cup quick oats

⅓ cup granulated sugar

¼ cup dark brown sugar

½ teaspoon salt

1 stick of cold unsalted butter

Preheat oven to 350 degrees. Clean the berries and put into a medium bowl. (Use any berries you like; I have even hulled and sliced strawberries in this recipe.) Add the lemon zest, juice, sugar, flour and cinnamon into a large bowl and stir. Let that sit and get all cozy and flavorful while you make the crumble.

In another medium bowl, combine the crumble ingredients except for the butter and stir. At the last minute, take your butter out of the fridge and cut into cubes and add to the dry crumble ingredients. I get my clean hands right in there and smash it all together, working the butter into the dry ingredients until it forms little pebbles. It will take you a couple of minutes, but using your hands works best.

Pour the berry mixture into small or large ramekins (I have used both) almost to the top. Then put a crumble layer on each ramekin, almost covering the berries.

Bake for 40-45 minutes. You will know when they are done once the crumble topping is a little brown and you see the berries bubbling.

It's best to have these baked at least an hour before you want to serve them. They can even sit in the fridge overnight if you want to make ahead for a party, warming them 15-20 minutes before serving in a 350 degree oven.

Homemade Apple Sauce

There are quite a few all "natural" apple sauce options out there, even some unsweetened ones, so I am not suggesting that a busy mom make homemade apple sauce very often. However, if you have a bunch of apples from apple picking, for instance (as I have on occasion), you need to get creative. This recipe only took 10 minutes of peeling and cutting and 20 minutes of cooking and there it was—homemade applesauce!

INGREDIENTS

1 cooking apple (like a Granny Smith)

2 eating apples (Fuji for example, anything with some sweetness)

1 ripe pear (make sure it is ripe)

Juice and zest of half an orange

½ teaspoon cinnamon

¼ teaspoon freshly ground nutmeg

2 tablespoons sugar

Pinch of salt

1 ½ tablespoons butter

Peel and chop the apples and pear into small pieces, avoiding the cores.

Once all of the fruit is ready to go, zest the whole orange, and juice half the orange (save the other half to serve to the crazy kid who turns down homemade applesauce). Pour the juice and the zest into a nice sized pan that has a lid, add the cinnamon, nutmeg, sugar, salt and the butter. Cook over medium heat until the butter is melted, stirring occasionally. Add your fruit and stir.

Cook on medium heat with the lid on for 20 minutes. Use an immersion blender or a regular counter-top blender to take out the lumps (unless you like lumps). Serve hot or stick it in the fridge for later.

This recipe works great and teaches our kids how food can go from the orchard to the table in many forms. When I served this, both boys and my husband loved it immediately! Score! My daughter wasn't sure about the lumps, even after I blitzed it with the immersion blender. But she is a very tough critic these days so I am not letting it get me down!

Tips

This is great as a side dish with pork dishes like schnitzel (page 47) or as a dessert. It also makes an amazing applesauce cake (page 102).

• • • • •

Grandma's Applesauce Cake

One of my childhood favorites was an applesauce cake my maternal grandma made. I can still taste the spicy moist cake and the tangy smooth cream cheese icing, and I always wanted to recreate that cake. My mom insists it had confectioners' sugar sprinkled on top, with cherries. Weird—the myth of the applesauce cake and we all have a different version in our minds! Still others in the family insist it was my great aunt, not my grandma, who was the baker in the family. Well....whoever

Continued on next page

This recipe is literally the inspiration for my initial family cookbook project—7 years ago now. The details below were recently found amongst my great aunt's things, so it is the closest I may ever get to grandma's cake. I encourage everyone who has recipes in their family that they love to write them down, type them up, or create your own cookbook or blog! Once a recipe is forgotten by one generation it is gone from the family forever, so make the time to write them down.

INGREDIENTS

½ cup butter

1 cup sugar

1 ½ cups applesauce (see page 100)

½ cup raisins

2 cups flour

2 teaspoons baking soda

1 teaspoon cinnamon

1 teaspoon nutmeg

½ teaspoon ground cloves

1 teaspoon salt

You can add other fruit (I would guess dried cherries or dates would work) or nuts (I added 1 cup finely chopped pecans, roasted for 4 minutes in the oven first)

Also optional: Add 1 tablespoon molasses.

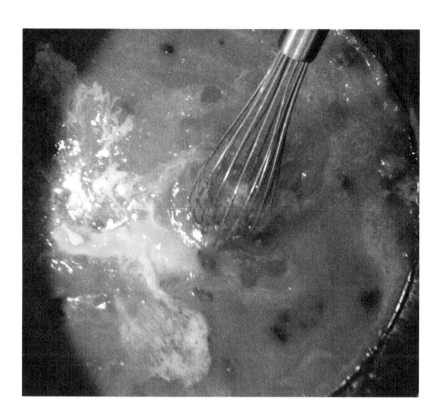

Continued from previous page

created the recipe, this one is very different than any other cake I have ever made. Bizarrely, it doesn't even have eggs in the batter —though my mom says it should; you can try it both ways and decide. I make this when we go apple picking in Septembers so the apples are literally right off of the tree. Grandma had apple trees in her yard that she used to make homemade apple sauce to use for this cake, fresh ingredients make all the difference.

Preheat oven to 350 degrees, then grease and flour a 9 x 13 inch pan. In a large pot, combine butter, sugar, applesauce and raisins and heat together, then cool.

Add all the rest of the ingredients. It will seem too dry, but as you stir it with a wooden spoon you will find it a very moist batter.

Pour into cake pan—either a Bundt pan or sheet pan will do. Cook for 40 minutes, then insert a toothpick into the center; if it comes out clean it's done; if it is really wet still, give it a bit more time.

Here's to documenting our family's history before our memories confuse them!

Serve with ice cream or whipped cream (see page 139) or just a fork.

Apple Turnovers

I love frozen puff pastry sheets and use it to top my chicken pot pie and to make garlic bread sticks, too. This recipe conjures up hot gooey pastries you can make at home—all you need are puff pastry sheets and a little imagination!

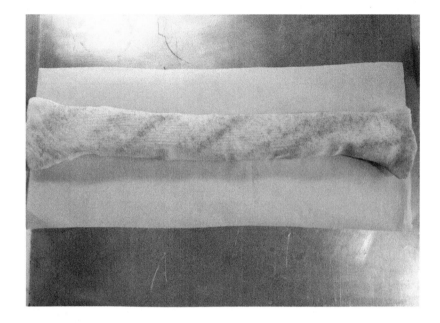

INGREDIENTS

Flour (only half a cup or so, just for the board)

Two sheets of puff pastry

2 tablespoons unsalted butter melted

Cinnamon sugar

¼ cup raisins

1 Granny Smith or Fuji apple, peeled and very thinly sliced

½ cup chopped pecans or walnuts, roasted 4 minutes at 350 degrees

¼ cup brown sugar

Preheat oven to 425. Put some flour on a cutting board and roll out one of the thawed puff pastry sheets. Brush the melted butter all over the top side, sprinkle the cinnamon sugar all over. On half the sheet lay the apple slices flat, then sprinkle over and around the apple: Nuts, raisins and brown sugar. Fold the other half of the puff pastry over the filling.

Once the top is covering the apple mixture, crimp the edges by pressing the tines of a fork down where the ends meet. Brush the top with more butter and sprinkle with more cinnamon sugar, then place on a parchment-covered baking sheet. Slide the baking sheet onto the middle rack of the oven and set a timer for 20 minutes.

Check the pastry, and if it is not browned and crunchy on top, set the timer for another 10 minutes. If still not browned, try one more 10 minutes and it should be done! Cool it for 20 minutes to allow it to set, then cut it into thick slices and serve.

For the other sheet, follow the same directions as above, including the butter, cinnamon sugar, and raisins, but instead of the apple and nuts

spread some good quality all natural black currant jelly as a filling. Tastes fantastic! Cook for 20–40 minutes as above, just making sure the top is browned before removing from the oven.

What other jellies, jams or thinly sliced fruits and nuts could you use to make this pastry? Answer: just be creative! How about some Nutella and raspberries? Maybe next time I will try that.

Great served as a breakfast treat, or add some homemade whipped cream (page 139) and it becomes an elegant dessert!

Tips

Don't roll it, or else the pastry that ends up in the middle will stay raw. I made that mistake so you don't have to—you're welcome!

· · · · ·

Kid's Yogurt Parfaits

INGREDIENTS

16 ounces of your favorite yogurt, divided among three glasses

Fresh fruit (cleaned blueberries, blackberries or raspberries, cleaned and sliced strawberries, round banana slices—or any combination)

Crunchy element (could be a layer of granola, a cookie, cheerios sprinkled on top, or chopped peanuts or pecans)

Squirt of whipped cream and/or swirls of chocolate or butterscotch syrup, home-made fruit sauces or a drizzle of honey (if the yogurt is a particularly tart Greek variety, mix in some honey to sweeten it)

A couple shakes of cinnamon for a boost of flavor

How does that saying go—necessity is the mother of invention? Over the years the kids have developed very different likes and dislikes, but they all enjoy yogurt (though go their own way when it comes to which flavors are their favorite).

Each week I buy a large container of vanilla yogurt (organic, Greek...I follow the sales prices!) and use it for customized parfaits. You can dress up the parfaits with any elements you have on hand, according to each child's taste. Or, you can just clean and cut the fruit and let the kids create their own parfait masterpiece!

What I did for the photo above, was take vanilla yogurt, mix in cinnamon, then add each kid's favorite fruit to the top. Then I drizzled on some Hershey syrup and added a Milano cookie.

Sometimes I layer the parfait—for instance, these could be the layers: Yogurt, Sliced strawberries, Yogurt, Granola, Whipped cream, Sliced strawberries or strawberry sauce (page 108) if you have some leftover.

This is a good way to create a healthy dessert and can be made with whatever you have on hand. Just think of balancing crunchy and smooth, as well as sweet and tart.

Grown-up Cherry Parfait

INGREDIENTS

1 cup of high quality 2% Greek yogurt

2 generous spoonfuls of sour cherry (I used Sarantis Greek Traditional Fruit Preserves)

1 generous tablespoonful of vanilla granola

1 fresh cherry for the top

My eldest, who has the taste buds of a sophisticated 40-year-old restaurant critic (who happens to be in the body of a grammar school kid) loves this, but the twins were skeptical. The flavor combination is a bit sophisticated, but I love it, too! This particular yogurt parfait tastes so great because the Greek yogurt is tart, but tastes richer and creamier against the cherry, which is even more tart. I also suggest a vanilla yogurt because cherry and vanilla are a classic combination. With yogurt being so good for us, this is a healthy treat for the family or a nice quick lunch.

Put half the yogurt in the bottom of a glass dish, then spoon on the cherry, cover with the remainder of the yogurt and top with granola and a fresh cherry. The contrast of flavors and textures makes this delicious!

Breakfast/Dessert Berry Sauces

Hot Blueberry Sauce

INGREDIENTS

1 pint of blueberries

Zest and juice of a large orange

¼ cup granulated sugar

2 shakes of cinnamon

1 teaspoon almond extract

Pinch salt

These are sauces we make to pour over pancakes or French toast. They would also make exceptional ice cream toppings!

Put all ingredients in a medium sauce pan and bring to a boil over a medium-high flame, stirring occasionally, for about 15 minutes. You will see the blueberries pop, transforming from a mound into a sauce (reminds me of how quickly cranberries turn into a sauce after adding sugar and applying heat).

Serve once it looks like a chunky sauce. If your kids are really picky, you can push it through a fine mesh sieve to take out the chunks (but the skins are a good source of fiber).

Strawberry Sauce

INGREDIENTS

8 whole strawberries

2 tablespoons confectioner's sugar

Pinch of salt

Juice of 1 lemon

My son made this today and used apple juice instead of lemon and threw in a handful of cleaned raspberries and a little bit of strawberry jelly. It came out great! Another time my son added a few frozen cherries and raspberries...still amazing!

Cut the hulls off of the strawberries and put them into a mini food processor or blender. Add confectioners' sugar, salt, and lemon juice.

Pulse until a sauce is formed.

Grilled Pineapple

I don't love pineapples on their own, although the smell of them is extraordinary, and I love them in shakes and pina coladas! Tonight we grilled them with honey and I loved it! It transformed them into a softer, sweeter version of themselves (kind of like me after a glass of red and a piece of dark chocolate!) One trick for choosing a good pineapple at the store is to get it when it's ripe (unless you won't need it for a while) by choosing one with a lot of yellow, that smells nice and has leaves that easily pull out from the top of the fruit.

Fast, easy and delicious, everything a busy family needs! Cut your pineapple by first taking off the skins, then slice 1 ½ inch slices, then take out the cores. Drizzle with honey on both sides and throw it on the grill. Warm both sides, getting those nice grill marks on them and pulling out the sweetness from the fruit. Before serving you can hit it with cinnamon, chocolate sauce and/or some chopped macadamia nuts. This may get your pickiest of eaters to try pineapple!

Primary Color Shake

INGREDIENTS

2 bananas (very ripe)

½ cup of blueberries (frozen or fresh...I freeze a ton of them when they are in season, since the price really jumps the rest of the year)

6–8 strawberries, cleaned, trimmed and cut (fresh or frozen)

½ cup of organic vanilla or banana yogurt, or Greek yogurt

1 cup of 1% milk

3 shakes of cinnamon

1 tablespoon honey

Put all ingredients in a blender; if you are using all fresh fruit (no frozen fruit), add 4 or 5 ice cubes. Mix with the "ice crush" feature for 10 seconds (you will hear the sound change when the cubes have been crushed), and then change to "mix" or "puree" for 10 more seconds. Serve in glasses with a large strawberry slice with a slit in it so you can hang it on the rim, or use a crazy straw to gain some fun points. Even add a little whip cream on top and call it dessert!

Secret # 1: Just about anything tastes good in a shake. You can hide all manner of healthy items or get decadent and throw in syrups and cookies and cake. Really, it is hard to go wrong.

 # 2: Don't give them ice cream shakes at home for a few years; that way they will believe fruit and yogurt shakes are the bomb!

 # 3: If the fruit you use is sour, like raspberries, add a bit of honey or a splash of sweet juice in the mix to counteract the sourness. When we have "Green Machine" or "Blue Machine" in the house we add those to shakes for added flavor and nutrition.

 # 4: Experiment and encourage your kids to invent new shakes as well!

My son invented this shake, which only makes sense—he is very creative and artistic and loves fruit! I have many fantastic shakes in my arsenal, and this is one of the best. My favorite shake was too boring for him, it is similar to this recipe but only has the bananas, yogurt, milk, cinnamon and honey. He needed to jazz it up!

Cantaloupe Shake

INGREDIENTS

Most of a cantaloupe, cut into cubes (reserve a quarter of it for eating)

Juice of a lime and half an orange (if all you have is a lemon, you can use juice of one lemon)

¼ cup sugar

1 cup cold water

2 cups ice

Mix all of the ingredients in a blender, first 20 seconds on "ice crush" (just listen for when the cubes have been thoroughly crushed), then on "puree" for 10 seconds. Serve immediately.

Kids love to make and drink shakes; in some cases, they will even drink what they won't eat. For example, my kids are more apt to drink this shake than to eat sliced cantaloupe. We love shakes so much that I keep my blender out on the kitchen table all the time, but especially in the summer shakes are popular in my house! This shake is very refreshing.

Tip

This must be served right after it is blended, or it will separate.

• • • • •

Tip for Mom & Dad

The adults can add some Midori melon liquor and vodka for a refreshing cocktail.

• • • • •

Tropical Shake

INGREDIENTS

2 cups frozen tropical fruit mix (or 1 cup fresh pineapple, ½ cup fresh slices of mango and ½ cup fresh trimmed strawberries)

1 cup pineapple juice

1 cup coconut water (or tap water)

2 small Greek yogurts (preferably mango coconut or pineapple flavor, but vanilla would also work)

We drink shakes all year round, but they make the most sense over the hot lazy days of summer. To honor the last day of the summer, I will share this shake that is particularly suited for Labor Day celebrations.

Tip

A fancy glass, umbrella, or straw can go a long way!

• • • • •

Tip for Mom & Dad

A little spiced or Malibu rum would work nicely with this shake to mark the end of summer (and a "Thank goodness school is starting again" toast while you're at it!).

• • • • •

Blend all of the ingredients on "ice crush" for 20 seconds, or until you can hear that the frozen fruit has been thoroughly crushed, then another 10 seconds on "puree." Pour into glasses and serve.

Variation: Grab one of those salad mixes with kale, chard and spinach and throw some in, just a few leaves the first time and see if you get away with it. But, make sure and replace the coconut water with a very sweet juice like apple or white grape juice to mask the vegetable flavors!

Peanut Butter Oat Shake

This tastes so great, and can provide the kids with a dessert that is full of protein and fiber. These flavors would taste just as wonderful if you added a banana or two, and a sprinkle of cinnamon. For kids with peanut allergies, replace the peanut butter with sun butter. Use your creativity!

INGREDIENTS

½ cup all-natural peanut butter

⅓ cup quick oats

4 scoops all-natural vanilla ice cream

1 ½ cups 1% milk

1–2 tablespoons chocolate syrup

Put all the ingredients into the blender. Blend on "stir" cycle or similar for 20–30 seconds. You want it to be thick like a milk shake at an old-fashioned diner.

Speculoos Shake

INGREDIENTS

½ cup Biscoff spread

1 cup of 1% milk

4 scoops of vanilla ice cream

1 teaspoon cinnamon

This is truly a dessert. I kept these ice cream-based shakes away from the kids for years, so they believed the fruit and yogurt version was a "real dessert." Once they hit third or fourth grade, though, they have tried it all so you might as well make some ice cream shakes at home. At least you can include an all-natural ice cream (I like Breyers all-natural vanilla, but whatever you choose always check to make sure it's actually "ice cream" not "dairy dessert").

Mix all the ingredients in a blender on the lowest setting, something like "stir" so you can keep it nice and thick. Serve with a Biscoff cookie and some all-natural whipped cream (page 139)! Delicious!

Variation: Nutella anyone??

Smoothie Pops

Once the weather warms up, our family loves to make ice pops. When my kids were little, I was forever looking for ways to provide desserts that would provide some nutrition, that was why I started getting them into ice pops. On many hot spring evenings, my kids can be found on the front steps hanging out and eating ice pops, chatting together. We always asked the kids to go outside to avoid spilling on the furniture. It became a tradition, so now we don't even have to ask them to go on the front steps when we make ice pops - they go right there automatically.

For years we would make our pops with strong, all natural juices. Favorite flavors include apple cider, orange juice (pulp free), pineapple juice and sometimes we mix juices and then pour them into the molds. Occasionally my eldest son likes to add a little surprise by dropping a blueberry or grape into the bottom of the pop.

This week my son came up with a new twist on our traditional pop - he made a batch with fruit smoothies, what a great idea! Any one of of the shakes I include in this book (or any other you can dream up) can be poured into the pop molds to create a rich and flavorful pop. Try primary color (page 111), tropical, or cantaloupe (page112-113) smoothies. Either make them at night for the next day, or in the morning and they will be ready for eating after dinner that night. Over the years we have bought molds from garage sales and also found a set at Bed, Bath and Beyond.

Nutrition on a stick, it doesn't get any sweeter!

Orangeade

INGREDIENTS

12 ripe oranges

Ice

1-2 tablespoons sugar

1 cup cold water

Clean all your oranges and slice them in half. Put ice in a large pitcher. Squeeze as much juice as you can out of each orange half and as the juicer fills, pour it into the pitcher over the ice through a mesh sieve if you want to avoid pulp. Once all the orange juice is in the pitcher, stir with a wooden spoon, add in 1 tbsp of the sugar and the cold water. Taste, and if it is a little bland, add in the other tbsp of sugar and stir again.

Serve with a big hearty breakfast. Jazz up the presentation by taking some big juicy strawberries, putting a slit into the middle of them and sticking them on the rim of the glass, or poke some grapes or blueberries on a toothpick and add it to the drinks.

Tip for Mom & Dad

Would taste amazing with a splash of cranberry juice, some seltzer and a shot of vodka.

· · · · ·

When I was at the Union Market in Washington, DC, I bought an orange juicer just like my Grandma used to have and decided this weekend to give it a go. I love milk glass, and this one that I bought is green milk glass and very pretty, and it was quite functional as well. I had my eldest son work with me to squeeze the oranges for fresh juice with breakfast on Sunday, it was a fun project. Not something I would ever dream of doing during the week, or when orange prices were high, but when I see those big bags of oranges for sale, I would definitely make this again. It took a lot of oranges to fill a pitcher for our family of 5, but it was so much fresher and tastier than any orange juice that comes from the grocery store!

Desserts

It might seem odd that after I spent so much time promoting fresh, wholesome ingredients that I bring in sweet and indulgent desserts. But really, it is very important to me to start with the idea that food brings us together and offers memories and traditions for the family; that is why dessert is so integral to balancing joy and health in family meals. A healthy dinner fills our bellies and warms our souls, while a scrumptious dessert leaves us all with a smile on our face.

I offer some desserts that are great for an elegant adult meal (see tiramisu, page 138 or chocolate decadent dessert, page 135) or for cooling down on a hot day (see shakes, page 111), and others you'll want to bring to picnics or barbecues, or sell at school bake sales. A great dessert is like the perfect, tender kiss at the end of an amazing date—you can't leave a family meal completely satisfied without a bit of sugar!

Nutty S'mores Bars

INGREDIENTS

2 sticks unsalted butter, melted, plus some to grease the pan

2 cups plain graham crackers (about 18 full crackers)

¼ cup sugar

½ teaspoon fine sea salt or kosher salt

3 cups milk chocolate chips

1 tablespoon coffee or espresso (optional)

3 ½ cups mini-marshmallows

½ cup crushed salted and roasted peanuts

This quick, one-pan dessert is just perfect for barbecues or to take to the beach! Everyone always begs for this recipe.

Tips

Best to cook chocolate slowly over a double boiler or else you may cause the chocolate to separate. Another option is to cook the chocolate in a microwave for 1 minute, then stir, then 30 second intervals stirring in between until melted.

• • • • •

Line a glass baking dish with aluminum foil. Preheat oven to 350 degrees.

In your food processor, grind the graham crackers into a fine meal. In a large bowl, combine your crumbs with the sugar, sea salt and melted butter. The mixture should look and feel like wet sand. Evenly press the crumb mixture into the bottom the foil-lined pan. Pop your crust into the oven and bake until it is golden brown, 11 to 14 mins. Remove the crust from the oven and allow it to cool in the pan.

Melt the milk chocolate in a double boiler with the coffee. Once the chocolate is fully melted, pour it over the cooled graham cracker crust. Spread the chocolate evenly over the crust with a butter knife. Sprinkle the marshmallows over the chocolate and press them lightly into the chocolate. Sprinkle the crushed peanuts over and in between the marshmallows so that you cannot see the chocolate peaking through the marshmallows. Preheat the broiler.

Broil the bars 6 inches from the flame until the marshmallows are golden brown, 1 to 2 minutes. Refrigerate the bars until the chocolate is hard, 2 hours or so. Grab the ends of the foil liner and lift the bars out of the pan in 1 piece. Move to a cutting board and cut into 12 large or 24 small squares.

Disappearing Nut Bars

INGREDIENTS

1 tablespoon soft butter for greasing the pan

12 graham crackers, crushed

1 teaspoon vanilla

1 stick plus 1 tablespoon melted butter

1 cup sweetened shredded coconut

½ cup white chocolate chips

½ cup butterscotch chocolate chips

1 cup dark chocolate chips

1 cup milk chocolate chips

1 ½ cup walnuts, chopped finely

½ cup pecans or almonds, chopped finely

1 can of sweetened condensed milk (14 ounces)

This is easy for kids to assemble and a house favorite. This is my take on the magic bars so often found at bake sales and school events. They can be done very quickly and are great for block parties or day trips. Always a crowd pleaser!

Preheat oven to 350 degrees. Grease a 9x9 glass pan with the softened butter. Crush the graham crackers in a food processor until they're the consistency of fine powder. Mix in the melted butter and vanilla until incorporated, and then press into the bottom of the pan.

Everything else is layered in order of the list above: First make a layer of coconut, then evenly layer the different types of chips and, lastly, the nuts. Finish off the bars by pouring the condensed milk evenly over the top.

Bake for 30 minutes, or until the milk is bubbling and browned around the edges. Let cool and then cut into squares when ready to serve.

Orange-scented Triple Chocolate Cookies

INGREDIENTS

2 sticks softened butter

¾ cup granulated sugar

⅔ cup brown sugar

Zest of 1 orange

2 tablespoons of orange juice

1 ½ teaspoon vanilla (I use Madagascar pure vanilla extract)

2 large eggs

2 ⅓ cup all-purpose flour

¾ cup baking cocoa

1 teaspoon baking soda

¼ teaspoon salt

1 cup white chocolate chips

1 cup semi-sweet chocolate chips

Preheat oven to 350 degrees. Cut parchment paper and place on four cookie trays.

Cream the butter and sugars in a standing mixer or in a large bowl with a handheld mixer. Once well combined, add the vanilla, orange zest, and orange juice. Add and combine eggs one at a time.

Put all the dry ingredients (flour, cocoa, baking soda, salt) in a small bowl and whisk together. Add the dry ingredients a little at a time while blending on low. Clean the sides and do a final mix with a spatula. Add the chips and blend.

Make the cookies all one size on each tray so they cook evenly. For small cookies, just drop about 1 ½ inches worth of dough and they will cook in 9–10 minutes. Medium are about 2 inches across and will cook in 13 minutes. Large cookies would be a 3-inch ball of dough and could take up to 15 minutes to cook. I like to do a tray of each size.

I started teaching my kids how to roll cookie dough when they could barely reach the top of the table. From ages 2-4 years old, more mess was created than finished cookies, but it was a fun way to keep them out of trouble and paved the way for their future successful efforts in baking. Now that they are big kids, they have real skill to make the dough balls uniform on each tray, and they can even follow a recipe and make the dough themselves (we always get a little math lesson in there as we double and triple the recipe). All we have to deal with these days are occasional motivation issues, but

Continued on next page

Orange-scented Triple Chocolate Cookies

Once cooked through, let them cool on the tray for a minute or two before laying them on a cooling rack. (This is where you'll be glad you opted to use the parchment paper!)

Store in an airtight container for a few days or freeze up to 30 days.

Tips

It is super easy to zest an orange, just use a micro-plane. Kids can help out once you show them how. My kids do —it's fun for them to participate and it saves me a little time.

Cut the parchment to size or a bit smaller than the trays. If you let the parchment hang over the side it will char and burn. You don't have to use parchment with this recipe, I just find it much more forgiving when removing the cookies from the trays and clean-up is a snap.

• • • • •

Continued from previous page

if you can get them off the electronics and onto the cookie trays, they invariably enjoy the task and absolutely gobble up the results! Who can resist a hot cookie right out of the oven? Not me!

Cherry Triple Chocolate Chip Cookies

These are similar to the orange-scented variety in the previous recipe, but feature dried cherries and coffee liqueur instead of the orange flavors. They got rave reviews the very first time out of the oven; the tart dried cherries worked well off of the extra sweet white chips, and the coffee liqueur make the chocolate taste even stronger.

INGREDIENTS

2 sticks softened butter

¾ cup granulated sugar

⅔ cup brown sugar

1 cup dried cherries

1 tablespoon coffee liqueur (Kahlua, for example)

1 ½ teaspoon vanilla (I use Madagascar pure vanilla extract)

2 large eggs

2 ⅓ cup all-purpose flour

¾ cup baking cocoa

1 teaspoon baking soda

¼ teaspoon salt

1 cup white chocolate chips

1 cup semi-sweet chocolate chips

Tips

Best eaten dunked in some cold milk.

• • • • •

Cherry Triple Chocolate Cookies

Preheat oven to 350 degrees. Cut parchment paper and place on four cookie trays.

Cream the butter and sugars in a standing mixer or in a large bowl with a handheld mixer. Once well combined, add the vanilla, dried cherries, and coffee liqueur. Add and combine eggs one at a time.

Put all the dry ingredients (flour, cocoa, baking soda, salt) in a small bowl and whisk together. Add the dry ingredients a little at a time while blending on low. Clean the sides and do a final mix with a spatula. Add the chips and blend.

Make the cookies all one size on each tray so they cook evenly. For small cookies, just drop about 1 ½ inches worth of dough and they will cook in 9–10 minutes. Medium are about 2 inches across and will cook in 13 minutes. Large cookies would be a 3-inch ball of dough and could take up to 15 minutes to cook. I like to do a tray of each size.

Once cooked through, let them cool on the tray for a minute or two before laying them on a cooling rack.

Aunt Joyce's Chocolate Chip Cookies

INGREDIENTS

2 sticks butter, softened

¾ cup sugar

¾ cup light brown sugar

1 tablespoon vanilla

2 tablespoons hazelnut liqueur

2 eggs

2 ½ cups all-purpose flour

1 teaspoon baking soda

½ teaspoon salt

2 cups milk chocolate chips (Aunt Joyce uses 4 cups, but I am not as brave!)

1 cup chopped pecans

1 cup chopped walnuts

Cream the butter, sugar, and brown sugar until well blended with a standing mixer or in a large bowl with a handheld blender. Mix in the Frangelico and vanilla until light and fluffy. Blend in 1 egg at a time.

Whisk together the flour, baking soda, and salt in a medium bowl. Add the flour mixture slowly into the wet ingredients. Blend well, then stir in the chocolate chips and nuts.

Refrigerate the dough for a few hours or overnight (this trick is probably why Aunt Joyce's cookies are thicker than mine!).

Preheat the oven to 325 degrees. Spread parchment paper on cookie trays and drop 1 teaspoon of dough for each cookie, 2 inches apart. Bake for 10–13 minutes.

Best served warm and gooey!

Tips

Always toast the chopped nuts in a 350 degree oven until you can smell them, about 4 minutes.

My Aunt Joyce sent these wonderful hazelnut chocolate chip cookies to us at Christmas time, complete with her recipe card. Thank you, Aunt Joyce! My chocolate chip cookies are usually much flatter—these were thick and had a lovely flavor (and it is always interesting to add a little liquor to a recipe). Aunt Joyce is one of my food mentors. She taught me at a very young age how home cooking and baking can make any occasion more special. I always make a few variations on chocolate chip cookies to fill out my holiday tins, they are fast but more than that they are a crowd pleaser!

Orange Iced Cookies

Chocolate is the core dessert around my house, but when putting together Christmas cookie tins I make sure to include different tastes so there is something for everyone. This cookie is the best of the citrus options; it really pops with flavor and the icing makes it very rich. Orange goes great with chocolate anyway, so let's just look at these as the compliment to the chocolate cookies in the tin, supporting the main event!

INGREDIENTS FOR COOKIES

2 cups all-purpose flour

¼ teaspoon baking soda

¼ teaspoon salt

1 ½ sticks unsalted butter (softened)

1 ¼ cup sugar

½ tablespoon orange zest

2 large egg yolks

1 teaspoon orange liqueur (or use orange extract)

1 cup confectioners' sugar

2–3 tablespoons fresh orange juice (squeeze it from the oranges you zested)

INGREDIENTS FOR ICING

1 cup confectioner's sugar

2–3 tablespoons orange juice (from the oranges you zested)

½ tablespoon orange zest

Zest your oranges to get the 1 tablespoon of zest and reserve in the fridge until you need it. Squeeze a couple of oranges to collect the 3 tablespoons of juice for the icing, and reserve this in the fridge as well. Whisk together the flour, baking soda, and salt.

Use a handheld mixer to blend the butter in a large bowl (or in the bowl of a standing mixer) on medium high for 1 minute or until smooth. Add the sugar and half a tablespoon of the orange zest and beat for another 2 minutes.

Beat in the egg yolks one at a time, then beat in the orange liqueur. Add the flour mixture slowly, beating on the lowest setting, until well combined and a soft dough has formed.

Scoop the dough in rounded tablespoons onto parchment-covered trays (I roll them a bit like a meatball into nice even orbs). Pop the trays into the freezer for at least 30 minutes, up to overnight. You need to bake them straight from the freezer, so when you are getting ready to bake the first batch, preheat the oven to 375 degrees.

Bake cookies for 15–17 minutes, until lightly browned around the edges. Place on cooling racks until room temperature, then ice.

To make the glaze: Whisk together the confectioners' sugar, 2 tablespoons of the juice and the 1/2 tablespoon of zest. If it seems too thick, you can add the last tablespoon of the juice.

Ice the cookies once cool, and leave to set on wire racks for an hour. Store immediately in an airtight tin for a few days or freeze for up to 1 month.

Tips

Depending on the thickness of the zest, to get the full tablespoon of zest could take as many as 4 or 5 oranges! Make sure you use the top orange layer of the skin only, that has all the flavor.

• • • • •

Back-to-School Brownies

INGREDIENTS

8 ounces semisweet chocolate baking bar

1 cup unsalted butter, cut into pieces

2 cups flour

½ teaspoon baking powder

1 teaspoon salt

1 teaspoon instant coffee (or 1 tablespoon espresso or coffee liqueur—in which case you can use the rest for chocolate-tinis!)

2 cups brown sugar

2 teaspoons vanilla

4 large eggs

⅔ cup semisweet chocolate chips

¾ cup roasted, chopped walnuts or pecans

Why do brownies remind me of school? They just seem like the perfect treat to fill a kid's tummy at 3:00, but still leave room for dinner.
They are such a versatile dessert, if done from scratch they would please both the pickiest kids and adults equally!
This recipe will taste so good you won't ever pick up those boxed mixes again.

Preheat oven to 350 degrees. Butter and flour a 9x13 inch lasagna pan.

Melt the chocolate bar and butter in a large saucepan over low heat, stirring until melted. Let cool to room temperature.

While the chocolate mixture is cooling down, chop the nuts and put them on a cookie tray in the preheated oven for 4-5 minutes.

Tips

Whenever I bake or cook with nuts, I roast them in the oven until you can smell their oils coming out. Roasted nuts will provide more flavor to a dish.

· · · · ·

Whisk together the flour, salt, and baking powder (and instant coffee if using) into a medium bowl. Once the chocolate mixture is cool, use a standing mixer or a handheld blender to mix in the brown sugar and vanilla. Blend in the eggs one at a time, then the liqueur if using.

Slowly blend the flour mixture into the chocolate a third at a time so the flour doesn't get lost in the air. Stir in chips and nuts. Pour into the greased pan and bake it in the center of the oven for 30-35 minutes. Cool and then "dress" the top with confectioners' sugar or frosting (I think these are best with the peanut butter frosting recipe that follows).

Peanut Butter Frosting

INGREDIENTS

1 cup confectioners' sugar

1 cup peanut butter

5 tablespoons softened unsalted butter

1 teaspoon real vanilla extract

⅓ cup heavy cream

Chocolate and peanut butter are such a sumptuous combination! This is a very straightforward recipe your kids could make themselves. Never buy that strange icing in a container from the store again (unless it is for a school event; the homemade icing doesn't store well). This particular recipe would not be suitable for school anyway, due to so many kids having a peanut allergy. Making icing at home is so easy, and the results are amazing. Give it a try and I don't think you will go back to the pre-made stuff.

Put the sugar, peanut butter, and butter into a large bowl and use a handheld mixer to blend until fully combined. Add the vanilla and heavy cream and blend until nice and smooth. Finish combining with a spatula and spread on cooled chocolate sheet cake, cupcakes (page 136), or brownies (page 132). You may need to double the recipe to fully ice a layer cake!

Chocolate Decadent Dessert

INGREDIENTS

1 ½ cups heavy cream

1 cup whole milk

½ cup sugar

1 teaspoon pure vanilla extract

1 teaspoon coffee liqueur or cooked espresso

8 ounces semisweet chocolate (or 8 ounces unsweetened chocolate and an extra half cup sugar)

6 large egg yolks

You have to really love chocolate (I do!) to appreciate this dessert. It is amazing but super rich, and a lot goes a long way so you can use small ramekins, only filled halfway, to get a wonderful dessert for guests or a special treat for the kids.

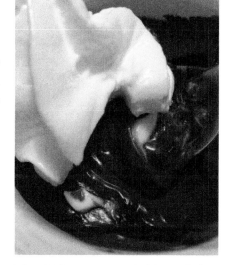

Preheat oven to 250 degrees. Chop the chocolate into small chunks. Pour the cream and milk into a medium pot and add the sugar, vanilla, and liqueur/espresso. Bring to a boil over medium heat, stirring frequently until boiling. Once you see the bubbles, add the chocolate and whisk until melted. Pull the pot off of the heat.

Lightly beat the egg yolks in a bowl. Temper them by stirring in about a tablespoon of the chocolate mixture, then pour into the chocolate mixture slowly while whisking constantly (this will allow the eggs to come up in temperature so you don't end up with scrambled eggs!).

Pour the mixture into ramekins, then place them into lasagna dishes or similar—anything with sides that will allow making a bain-marie.*

Bake on the center rack for 1 hour 15 minutes. You can tell they are ready, once the center is just a bit jiggly. Cool to room temperature then refrigerate and serve cold.

Serve with homemade whipped cream (page 139) and something to offset the richness. Fresh raspberries or strawberries, or some crushed cashews would be great accompaniments!

Tips

Always go for high-end chocolate, especially when it is the star of the show like in this recipe.

• • • • •

"Bain-marie" is when you cook something in the oven gently, by filling a casserole dish with cold water, halfway up the sides of the ramekins. Once all of the filled ramekins are in the dish and the cold water is halfway up the sides of the dishes, cover with aluminum foil and carefully slide into the oven. You want to avoid splashing the water into the chocolate custards while putting the dishes into the oven, and later when removing the dishes from the oven.

Vanilla Cupcakes with Chocolate Ganache

Cupcakes were huge during 2010–2013, with all the TV shows celebrating these mini-cakes, and they became more and more available with such cool flavor combinations, both sweet and savory. But I enjoy the giving the people what they want, and for a birthday party with a group of kids vanilla will always work. We have made these vanilla cupcakes and a few different icing choices and let the kids ice and decorate the cupcakes themselves. For one party, we made it a decorating contest with little prizes from the Dollar Store or Five Below and the kids loved the competition as well as eating their masterpieces.

INGREDIENTS

1 ½ cups self-rising flour

1 ¼ cup all-purpose flour

2 sticks of unsalted butter, softened

2 cups granulated sugar

4 large eggs

1 cup of whole milk

1 ½ teaspoons vanilla extract (or, for an even more natural taste, scrape the inside of a vanilla bean into the batter and add just ½ teaspoon of vanilla extract)

Soften the butter and put the milk and eggs on the counter to get them to room temperature.

Preheat oven to 350 degrees.

Mix the flours in a small bowl and place the milk and vanilla into another small bowl or pourable Pyrex measuring cup. Cream the butter for a couple of minutes in a standing mixer or in a large bowl with a handheld mixer, then add the sugar gradually and beat together for another 3 minutes until fluffy.

Beat in each egg one at a time. Then, as you do with cake recipes, alternate adding the milk/vanilla mix and the flours one third at a time, starting and ending with the milk. Do not overbeat; you are looking for the batter to just be combined, scraping down the bowl sides and bottom with a rubber spatula to make sure you got all the flour incorporated into the mix.

Spoon the batter into cupcake liners. Do not fill to the top; leave about a quarter of the cup empty to allow for rising. Bake for 20–25 minutes until a toothpick comes out clean from the center of the cupcake.

Tips

If you don't have much time to soften the butter, cut it into small 1 tablespoon chunks on a plate and it will soften in 10–15 minutes.

• • • • •

Chocolate Ganache Frosting

INGREDIENTS

½ or 1 cup heavy cream

8 ounces of good quality dark chocolate

Pinch of sea salt

Optional: 1 teaspoon of coffee liqueur

Chop the chocolate into 1-inch pieces, and put into a medium bowl. Heat the heavy cream (and coffee liqueur, if using) over medium heat, using 1 cup for thinner frosting to drizzle or ½ cup if you want it to be thicker as a topping. Once you start seeing bubbles on the edges of the cream, it is ready to pour onto the chocolate in the bowl. The hot cream will melt the chocolate without having to put the chocolate on direct heat, which makes it break and split; this is a gentle way to keep the chocolate's texture perfect.

Add the pinch of salt, then stir constantly with a whisk until it is melted. Once it is shiny and smooth, you are good to go. Try not to eat it all right out of the bowl!

Tips

Let it cool a bit, and then take each cupcake and frost it by holding upside down over the ganache and dipping it top first into the chocolate and pulling it right out. This is the best way to get an even coating.

• • • • •

Tiramisu

INGREDIENTS

1 cup heavy cream

5 tablespoons sugar

4 egg yolks

1 pound mascarpone cheese

7 ounces sponge lady finger cookies (which may be tough to find, but most grocery stores stock them in summer in the produce section)

4 tablespoons strong espresso

5 tablespoons amaretto

Cocoa powder to garnish the top

Whip the cream and 1 tablespoon of the sugar until stiff. Mix the egg yolks with the rest of the sugar on the highest speed of a hand mixer until creamy. Add the mascarpone in spoonfuls, then stir in the cream using a lower mixer speed.

Put a few lady fingers aside for decoration, and then take half of the rest and line a glass lasagna pan or glass trifle dish.

Combine the espresso and amaretto, then trickle half of it over this layer of fingers. Then spread half of the cream as the next layer. Do one more layer of lady fingers covered with the amaretto/espresso mixture, then a final layer of cream.

Top the tiramisu with the decorative lady fingers, and sprinkle with cocoa powder. Leave to stand in the refrigerator for at least 1 hour before serving.

This dessert is cool and light—perfect for summer— but it packs a punch. It's also for the adults only because it contains alcohol that is not cooked out, and tons of caffeine. I don't know about you, but my kids have enough natural energy without giving them caffeine! Offer an alternative for young eaters.

Silky Whipped Cream

INGREDIENTS

1 eight ounce container mascarpone cheese (usually near the Brie in the fancy cheese section at the grocery store).

1 cup heavy cream

1 teaspoon vanilla

⅓ cup confectioners' sugar

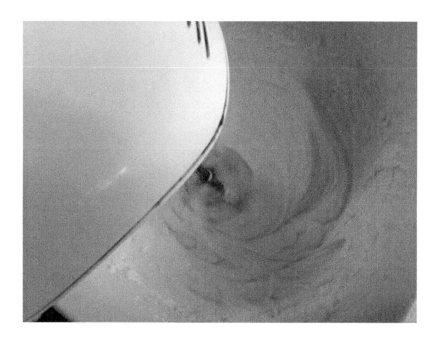

For summer desserts that are light and delicious, from fresh fruit cups (page 96) and crumbles (page 98) to tiramisu (page 138), the best part can be the topping—especially if you use this rich version of homemade whipped cream. For the kids, you may want to up the sugar, unless what you are topping is already very sweet; then the best way to balance it out will be to have the whipped cream less sweet. It is hard to go wrong with whipped cream!

Using a handheld blender or standing mixer, whip all four ingredients until thick and fluffy. You should see trailing lines in the cream, as in the photo above. Don't over whip or the cream might "break." If this happens, add another half cup of cream and try again.

Luscious, rich and velvety, you will never use the store-bought chemical filled version again.

Tips for The Adults

You can flavor this basic recipe by adding a tablespoon of your favorite liqueur or Bailey's Irish Cream (yum!).

• • • • •

Best Banana Muffins

INGREDIENTS

4 large bananas (2 cups when smashed)

⅔ cup vanilla yogurt (I use organic low fat vanilla or banilla flavor)

3 cups all-purpose flour

1 cup whole-wheat flour

4 tablespoons baking powder

1 teaspoon baking soda

½ teaspoon salt

½ teaspoon ground nutmeg

1 teaspoon cinnamon

Grated zest of 2 large oranges

½ cup chopped walnuts toasted (see Tip on next page)

1 cup chocolate chips (we used mixed dark, milk and white chocolate last time, since that is what we had in the house)

4 large eggs

1 ½ cups firmly packed golden brown sugar

12 tablespoons unsalted butter, melted

1 cup whole milk

OPTIONAL TOPPINGS

½ cup *Demerara sugar or sweetened coconut flakes

Position 2 racks in the middle of the oven, and preheat to 350. Butter and flour muffin tins or two 9x5 inch loaf pans if you prefer making bread. I made 12 large muffins and 24 mini muffins using the above portions, just half the ingredients if you need to make less. It is a bit of effort so I figure I will make a bunch of them, some for now, save some in the freezer for later and give some away!

In a small bowl (I use a 4 cup Pyrex measuring cup), using a fork, mash the bananas. You should have 2 cups. Add the yogurt into the bananas.

In a separate medium sized bowl, stir together the all-purpose and whole wheat flours, baking powder, baking soda, salt, nutmeg, cinnamon, orange zest, nuts and chips. Set aside.

In a large bowl combine the eggs, brown sugar, butter and milk with a handheld blender. Beat on medium-low speed just until blended. Add the dry ingredients in 3 batches alternately with the banana mixture and blend on low speed just until combined. Do not over mix.

Before I had the kids, and it was just my husband and I, we were always sitting on over-ripe bananas with black spots all over them and no one to eat them – so banana bread was almost a weekly event. That has all changed recently. Now I buy a bunch of bananas and they move pretty quickly between cut fruit and shakes. However, I now have a new appreciation for small snacks to give the kids for day trips and in school lunches. So I updated the bread recipe and I create yummy muffins by adjusting some of the ingredients. It can work for bread or muffins now and is more of a sweet and healthy treat.

Best Banana Muffins

Pour the batter into the prepared pans filling about 3/4 the way to the top of the muffin pans, and if making bread then smooth the top with the rubber spatula. For a cool topping sprinkle Demerara sugar that will caramelize during baking or sweetened coconut that will get golden brown.

Bake until toothpick inserted into the center comes out clean.

Mini muffins: 15-17 minutes

Large muffins: 25-27 minutes

Bread: 55-60 minutes

Transfer to a wire rack and let cool in the pans for 5 minutes, then turn out onto the rack and cool completely. For the muffins, run a thin butter knife around the edges to help coax them out.

Store in an airtight container at room temperature for 2-3 days or freeze for up to 1 month. Makes a great gift for a sick friend, good for bake sales or a nice surprise for helpers in your life (think babysitters, house cleaners, teachers). Craft stores now carry bakery boxes with clear tops that are very decorative, usually used for cupcakes. You can fit 4 large muffins instead and it makes a nice little treat for someone who appreciates homemade gifts.

*Demerara Sugar

Here is some info on Demerara sugar (you should find it in your local store in the baking aisle): "Demerara" is a light brown, partially refined, sugar produced from the first crystallization during processing cane juice into sugar crystals, but unlike brown sugar, it does not include molasses. It adds a nice crunch to the top of baked goods in the US, and in England it is frequently used to sweetened tea and coffee.

Tip

Just put the walnuts on a cookie tin in the preheated oven for 4 minutes, then cool them. It brings out the flavor.

• • • • •

My Favorite Banana Cake

INGREDIENTS

2 Sticks of softened butter

2 cups sugar

4 large eggs

2 cups mashed ripe bananas

2 ½ cups self rising flour

½ teaspoon cinnamon (optional)

1 cup chopped walnuts

1 cup milk chocolate chips (tossed in 1 tbsp flour so that they don't sink to the bottom of the cake)

Preheat the oven to 350⁰. Grease a bundt pan with softened butter and then coat with flour thoroughly. Blend the sugar and butter in a KitchenAid® blender bowl or in a large bowl with a hand held mixer. Add the eggs 1 at a time, mixing well between additions. Mix in the bananas, then add the flour and cinnamon while blending on lowest setting. Mix in the walnuts and the flour covered chocolate chips with a spatula or wooden spoon.

This is a wonderful cake to make when you have over ripe bananas hanging around the fruit bowl. I often make this cake to bring to parties. Work time is only 20 minutes, then an hour in the oven, 10 minutes to cool and you can add the glaze and go.

Pour the batter into the bundt pan and put the cake in the middle of the oven. Cook for 55 minutes and check if a toothpick comes out clean. If not, then bake for 5 minute intervals and checking again.

Cool the cake for 15 minutes in the pan. While cooling, put all the glaze ingredients into a medium bowl and whisk. Set aside until the cake is on the plate.

Put a knife around the outside of the pan to loosen the cake from the pan. Invert onto a cake plate. Bang the top all over with a butter knife to loosen. Cross your fingers, then dump the cake out. Sprinkle confectioners sugar on top with a fine mesh sieve or cover with orange glaze as explained below.

Orange Glaze: 1 cup confectioners sugar, splash vanilla, zest of one orange and 1-2 tablespoons of milk, depending on how runny you like it. All ingredients are just combined with a whisk or hand held blender, starting off with 1 tablespoon milk and then adding in a bit more until it is thin enough to drizzle on top of the cake and it will slide down the sides.

Secret

I have to be honest; sometimes it comes out beautifully, other times not so much. For my run through and photo session, the cake did NOT come out well, so I patched it together and threw on the glaze. It looked funky so you are seeing a photo before I put it onto the cake plate. Even looking imperfect the flavors were all there so no harm done.

• • • • •

Busy Family Pantry Items

My dear friend Christie, like most of us, has a lot of balls in the air. She is a multi-talented woman with tons of creativity and drive in her career, is balancing being super mom to her two gorgeous girls, and being a supportive wife - but still finds time to help me out. Since I started my Blog, she has been an important adviser to me, and since her favorite place is not in the kitchen she is also sort of my target audience. She has gone on food adventures with me (here we are in Little Italy drinking our complimentary red wine, yum) and gave me some great ideas for content, including to make this article, smart lady.

What is it Oprah said? Everyone should have a Gale...well mine is Christie. She has been my cheer leader through thick and then, and the first idea she gave me for my Blog, was that if I am speaking to moms and dads who don't naturally gravitate towards cooking (but who want to make the effort for

Busy Family Pantry Items

their kids) start at the beginning and let them know what staples they need in their pantry. If someone is not a natural cook, things like what to stock can seem overwhelming; and, to simplify that will help them get organized. So here are the foods you will find in my pantry, on most random weekends when I am ready to cook.

These are the items I have in my pantry so I am ready for anything:

- Olive and canola oil
- Balsamic and apple cider vinegar
- Boxed chicken and beef broth (although I like to make it myself sometimes, it's not always practical)
- Tube of tomato paste, can of whole tomatoes and a few cans of crushed tomatoes (San Marzano are the best)
- Slivered almonds
- Onions, shallots and garlic
- Russet potatoes
- Jellies made with natural ingredients
- Natural peanut butter
- Hazelnut spread
- Hard and soft taco shells
- Dried pasta (the kids like trio pasta, I love the spaghetti that appears to have gotten a perm; officially called fusilli lunghi bucati). Also, I usually stock whole-wheat or high-fiber linguini, spaghett and angel hair as well as penne and ziti.
- Extra-wide egg noodles for goulash and casseroles
- All natural macaroni and cheese boxes for a quick weekday night side dish
- Elbow and fusilli pasta for making homemade mac & cheese
- Rice—arborio for risotto, and my favorite regular rice is a blend of white and brown with flaxseed that cooks in 20 minutes
- Wondra flour
- Plain bread crumbs and panko bread crumbs (it seems really easy to make your own, but I don't have time)

Busy Family Pantry Items

Dried spices and seeds, including:

- Cinnamon
- Cloves
- Ginger
- Allspice
- Cinnamon sticks
- Chili powder
- Mustard powder
- Nutmeg (ground or whole nutmeg)
- Paprika
- Old Bay Seasoning (for fish)
- Caraway seeds
- Garlic salt (a co-worker of mine told me once that a real cook would never use this, well, I am a mom first and it tastes great on pizza!)

Dried herbs:

- Thyme (great with ground meat dishes)
- Oregano
- Italian seasoning
- Bay leaves
- Herbs de Provence (lovely on roasted chicken/potatoes/root veggies)

Basics: Lemon pepper, ground pepper and whole peppercorns, sea or kosher salt, regular salt for baking (think the lady with the umbrella), baking soda, baking powder, cream of tartar, packets of plain gelatin, packets of yeast.

Booze to cook with: Marsala wine, dry sherry, white (dry) vermouth, vodka (for sauce, yes,but also to bribe the dishwasher), dark or amber beer, like Guinness or one of the new IPAs on the market, for stews (can also help to bribe the dishwasher) and red and white table wines.

For baking: Unsweetened and semisweet bars of chocolate, cocoa powder, chocolate chips, sweetened coconut flakes, graham crackers, mini-marshmallows, flour, self-rising flour, sugar, brown

Busy Family Pantry Items

sugar, confectioners' (icing) sugar, honey, real maple syrup, molasses, vanilla (Madagascar if you can but definitely only get the real vanilla, avoid "imitation vanilla" what is that anyway?), almond extract, raisins, quick oats, walnuts, almonds and pecans.

Booze for baking with: Chocolate liqueur (add to all sorts of chocolate desserts to bring out the bitterness in the chocolate), cherry brandy and hazelnut liqueur).

Stuff to have on hand for impromptu picnics and day-trips:
Granola bars, apple sauces, boxes of raisins, nuts, pretzels, all-natural juice boxes and organic milks.

For surprise guests:
Tortilla chips and natural salsa, whole grain crackers (great with a smoked gouda or herb brie), cashews, mixed nuts and some type of kid's snack like Pirate's Booty or Skinny Popcorn.

Substitutions, Exchanges and Additions

Conversions, Exchanges, Substitutions and Additions

With my simple arsenal of quick dinners and easy home baking, there are a bunch of tricks I know when it comes to conversions and ingredient swapping or additions. This is by no means an exhaustive list, just a few examples that have helped me along the way.

I am a big advocate of doubling recipes whenever you can, whether cooking or baking. Making things from scratch is a commitment, so why not make enough for this week, for next month and some to give away while you're at it? It may take a bit more effort but you will enjoy the results. When you are doubling or tripling a recipe, it helps to understand how to convert measurements.

Handy conversions:

16 cups = 8 pints = 4 quarts = 1 gallon

4 cups = 2 pints = 1 quart

2 cups = 1 pint

3 teaspoons = 1 tablespoon

4 tablespoons = ¼ cup

There are times when I don't have all the exact ingredients for a recipe and there's no time to run to the store (or wait for my lovely husband to run to the store for me) so there are a few substitutions that have come in handy in a pinch. I also look for ways to boost the nutrition in my baking and there are a couple of seamless ways to add some fiber to my yummy desserts.

Dairy: I have substituted milk one fatness level down in recipes without significant differences in flavor or texture. For instance, if you are told to use cream, you can use half and half (consisting of half cream half milk). Or, instead of half and half, you can use whole milk; instead of whole milk use 2% milk, etc. I just wouldn't jump too far down the list unless you have no choice. For instance, penne vodka is best with some heavy cream, but would still be rich and lovely with half and half. I just wouldn't make it with skim or 1% and expect good results. Buttermilk can be substituted with whole milk; just squeeze a lemon into the milk that will create that same effect that buttermilk has of being a bit curdled.

I refuse to cook with fat-free dairy; the fat-free cheese will not melt properly and the flavor and texture is sacrificed. Dairy has to have some fat in it if you ask me, or what is the point? Part skim cheeses work well for recipes, just don't ever go fat free!

Substitutions, Exchanges and Additions

Cookie healthy exchanges and additions: For most cookie recipes I will exchange the flour for whole wheat flour, but only ½ a cup of the total flour in the recipe (unless I double the recipe; then I will exchange 1 cup worth of the all-purpose flour for whole wheat). For chocolate chip cookies I throw in a handful of bran; no one ever notices the difference, and I have been able to provide a bit more fiber in a dessert—win-win!

Chocolate: When it comes to making cookies, use any kind of chips you want to try and you can't go wrong. But for chocolate recipes you need to stick to what the recipe calls for or make an equal substitution to get proper results:

- 2 ounces semisweet chocolate = 1 ounce unsweetened chocolate + 1 tablespoon granulated sugar

- Bittersweet and semisweet chocolate can be used interchangeably.

- 1 ounce Dutch processed cocoa = 3 tablespoons unsweetened cocoa powder plus ⅛ teaspoon baking soda

Onions: Although Vidalia onions are a bit sweeter and purple onions a bit more mild, I wouldn't worry about substituting either in any of my recipes for a regular yellow onion, if that is all I had. Shallots are my favorite, so I use them frequently with eggs, sauces and gravies. If I only had a yellow onion, I could easily use that instead of shallots in any of my recipes though; they are similar enough.

Herbs: Fresh herbs are all very different. For poultry, you can use any of the herbs found in those poultry mixes at the store: thyme, rosemary, sage…or even lemon thyme (which grows like crazy in my garden all summer and adds a nice hint of lemon to chicken or potatoes). Because I don't love cilantro (a very polarizing herb) I will use a flat leaf parsley instead in some recipes, but would never recommend switching cilantro in a recipe that requires parsley that is horrible! I did that by accident once, grabbing cilantro instead of parsley at the store and putting it in my Italian tomato sauce. Disaster. Also, when substituting dry herbs for fresh herbs, cut the measurements at least in half because dried herbs pack more flavor. Dried herbs also can be added early in the cooking, while fresh herbs need to be added at the end of cooking to avoid them turning black and losing their flavor.

Tips

Don't store your potatoes and onions near each other or the potatoes will rot quickly.

Store nuts in the freezer for a longer shelf life.

• • • • •

Desert Island Tools

There are so many kitchen tools out there, it can become overwhelming. So I decided to come up with my top 15 heavy hitters for hand tools and top 15 pieces of equipment that I would want if stuck on a desert island. I have a lot of other "stuff" filling my terribly cramped, old-fashioned kitchen, but these are the gems that I take out every week and couldn't live without!

Pull from this list when shopping for a wedding shower or engagement party for a couple who don't know what they are doing in the kitchen. Pick a couple desert island items and pair them with a simple cookbook (like this one maybe, or some of your family recipe cards for an added personal touch). I have packaged up some of my top picks and included some of my typed up recipes and it has gone over really well.

The thing is, you don't know what you need until you know what you are doing in the kitchen, and we all have to start somewhere. A little advice and encouragement can go far, and help the couple avoid wasting money on three different serving spoons and four whisks, when one good whisk, a carrot peeler, wooden spoon, and spatula will get them so much further.

Desert Island Tools

TOP FIFTEEN DESERT ISLAND KITCHEN TOOLS

1. **Carrot peeler**: Not just for carrots, but also fruit, butternut squash, potatoes, ginger and more

2. **Paring knife**: I use this all the time, probably even in situations when I "should" use a larger knife!

3. **Can opener**: We don't eat much canned soup but we do need to open up our crushed tomatoes and white beans!

4. **Microplane**: Perfect for zesting citrus fruits, grating chocolate, whole nutmeg and parmesan cheese.

5. **French whisk**: This is my favorite type; it has coils around a loop; a medium size whisk is also useful if that's what you can find. Perfect for eggs, combining dry ingredients for baking, and getting the lumps out of sauces and gravy (see photo on page 154).

6. **Hard plastic spatula**: For hamburger flipping, as well as taking the cookies off the pan and turning meats, home fries, potato pancakes, or grilled cheese (and anything and everything, really.)

7. **Rubber spatula**: Nothing is better for folding scrambled eggs or meringues, and cleaning the sides of the bowl when making batters; it also comes in handy for making sure the tops of pies and frosted cakes are evenly covered.

8. **Wooden spoon**: For stirring and serving soups, chilis, sauces, stews and combining batters, crumbles and anything you cook in a pot!

9. **Dry cup measures and spoon measures**: Cooking really can be done without these, but not baking.

10. **Pyrex small and large liquid measuring cups (1 cup and 4 cup versions)**: Ideal for heating milk and chocolate in the microwave, separating eggs or cracking eggs one at a time for batters, They can handle hot or cold and don't break easily, I even use them to microwave my only favorite frozen veggie, baby peas.

11. **Cork Screw**: How can one cook with booze without this?

12. **Lemon "Juicer"**: I like the old fashioned kind in the picture above right, the first one I found was wooden at a garage sale, they work great to get the most juice out of any citrus fruit (see photo on page 154).

13. **Thin Cake spatula**: This one is good for icing and cutting cakes (see photo on page 154).

14. Tongs: I grab them all the time for everything from meatballs to frying perogies to grabbing things that fall behind the piano. Great invention!

15. Large plastic spoon or ladle: Either will do, but you need something that scoops soups, stews and chili out quickly when serving or putting portions away in the freezer.

Honorable mentions: Serrated knife, for cutting nice crusty bread and tomatoes as well, **cake server**, **rubber brush** for basting and egg washing, **rolling pin** for cutter cookies, rolling puff pastry and pie crusts, and a second **rubber spatula** always helps.

TOP 15 COOKING AND BAKING DESERT ISLAND EQUIPMENT

1. Steamer pot: With vegetable and pasta baskets.

2. Nonstick pan: Perfect for pancakes and eggs.

3. Cast iron pan: Anytime you want something to get delicious and caramelized on the outside, you must use a cast iron pan; it works wonders for scallops, chicken, chops, burgers, etc. When you want the lovely brown bits for sauces, use this instead of a nonstick pan.

4. Dutch oven: As with the cast iron pan, great to caramelize the outside of meat and fish. The advantage with this is that after you've seared your short ribs or pot roast in it, you can just pop the lid on and slide the whole thing right into the oven. It works wonders on low temperatures to slow cook the meat until it falls off the bone. When cooking on the stovetop, it conducts heat very evenly. It is a

Desert Island Tools

game changer and if you haven't used one before, it's worth the investment. I recommend a large one if you have a family. You'll love it!

5. Medium Soup pot: Perfect for reheating food or serving up small portions, or cooking sauces.

6. Large stock pot: I always make large portions of homemade soup and sauces to freeze some for future weeks; a large stock pot is the perfect vessel. Large stock pot will also work well to boil corn, make chilis and all kinds of big pot foods to feed your family when the kids start eating you 'out of house and home' as teenagers.

7. Nesting bowls: Absolute essentials for cooking and baking. I prefer stainless steel or plastic. Ceramic look pretty but the bowls are too bulky and breakable for my crazy kitchen, glass bowls work well as an alternative and make for nice vessels to serve fruit salads.

8. KitchenAid standing mixer: A luxury, but if you bake as much as I do it is a lifesaver. If you cook more than you bake, don't bother. Any handheld mixer will do for occasional baking and for making such side dishes as mashed potatoes.

9. Cuisinart Mini-Prep: I use this every week! Sometimes I am feeling virtuous and I do all the chopping myself, but mostly I am in a mad dash to get stuff on the table and this tool is perfect to chop nuts, dice onions or pulverize carrots and celery to sneak into soups and stews. It can even save you time by

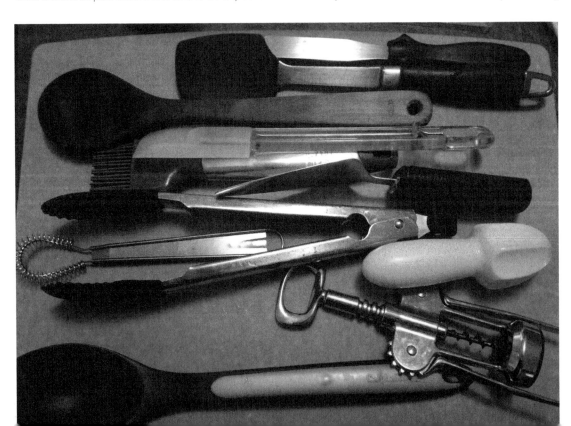

grating your parmesan or grinding oats into small pieces for challenging eaters. This is a miracle worker in the kitchen when it comes to time savings and much easier to clean than a full-size Cuisinart, so I almost never bother taking that one out of storage and use the Mini-Prep exclusively.

10. Cookie trays: I call these "not just for cookies trays" because if you get the type with small sides all around they work well to cook bread sticks, rolls, roast veggies and protect your stove from drips when cooking quiches or crumbles by catching the spills. (I think you'd ask for a jelly roll pan when shopping. For cookies I prefer the flat, light cookie trays with one or two side bent up for easier handling, but the other sides are flat to allow air to circulate and brown the cookies evenly.

11. Cooling racks: As with the above cookie trays, the primary purpose may be for cooling cookies, but there are dozens of other uses including cooling sweet and savory pies, cakes and tarts.

12. Lasagna dish: Not only for lasagna, this is also another good vessel for roasting veggies or making all manner of casseroles (noodle, sweet potato, etc.).

13. Produce and meat cutting boards: I have separate ones to avoid cross contamination. Look for two different styles or colors so you know which is which.

14. Pie dishes: These are pulled out frequently for quiches, meat pies, chicken pot pies and dessert pies.

15. Pasta bowl set: Comes with a large serving bowl and four flat bowls. I love to use the flat bowls when dipping schnitzel and other breaded meats and veggies, using one bowl for flour, one for egg and one for breadcrumbs. Also great to roll cookies into sugar or cinnamon sugar and of course for their intended use of serving pasta. The large serving bowl can double as a fruit bowl when not in use to serve a big pasta dinner.

Index

Index

Index

CPSIA information can be obtained at www.ICGtesting.com
Printed in the USA
BVOW07s0950131115

426976BV00002B/2/P